Anoroc- Tres

Anoroc- Tres

Deception Series

DORIAN SNOWDEN

Notion Press Media Pvt Ltd

First Published by Notion Press 2024
Copyright © Dorian Snowden
All Rights Reserved.
ISBN-13: 979-8896102649
ISBN-13: 979-8896106227

Made with ❤ on the Notion Press Platform

www.notionpress.com

Also by Dorian Snowden,

Derick Abraham series

Intruder

Nepolian series

Finally on my Nepolian

--

A Lost Nepolian Diary

Deception series

2020- I	*Anoroc: Uno*	2021- I
2020- II	*Anoroc: Duo*	2021- II
2020- III	*Anoroc: Tres*	2021- III
2020- IV		2021- IV

Novella

Anamika

Contents

Preface

Hai reader! *'Anoroc: Tres'* is the final book in *'Deception series'*. Chronologically this is the first book which I started in this series. I didn't have an idea of publishing this book while I was writing those down. I was just looking at the headings and news which I wanted, all my focus was on *'Anoroc: Uno'* and *'Anoroc: Duo'*. While I was somewhere in my second editing of previous books I decided on publishing so that the main news I collected can be easily put forward to the readers.

Acknowledgments

I wanted to thank each and everyone who cooperated in this series, Akshay, Anandu, Aravindan, Prahil, keeping their work aside and joining in with me, which wasn't easy for them, but they did for me.

Special thanks to Prahil for helping me with the book cover.

Author's Note

'*Anoroc: Tres*' is the third in the series. The pieces of information in this book are all the current updates that came on the news and other social media platforms which I wrote down and decided to put in one book, so that few of my posts in '*Anoroc: Duo*' can make sense to the sceptical readers.
Thank you!

ANOROC- TRES

2020

24th January

- On 31st December a guy in Wuhan went to the nearest hospital with difficulties in breathing, talking properly, severe heartache and suffocation.
    - → Doctors did further study and got shocked and fearful; the reason was, none of the doctors knew what disease he had.
    - → From the blood samples it became evident that he got attacked by some virus. Doctors got scared because they didn't have any vaccine and they were dealing with that virus for the first time.
    - → The doctors found out that the virus belongs to the Corona family and SATS which came earlier in early 2,000 and that killed around 774 people (it was hard to survive at that time).
- Scientists have discovered 6 types in the Corona family and they were on the earth for more than 10 thousand years. This can affect almost all animals and birds.
- Covid-19 is the 7th on the list and no one knows how to prevent it or know what to do with it. The scientist hasn't studied yet.
- 31st December was when the first case of the 7th generation Corona was reported.

- In just 20 days it spread all over the globe. Almost 600 people were affected, 20 dead worldwide. From China it went straight to America then Thailand and Indonesia.
- Two Indians were kept separate in Mumbai airport for analysing whether they were affected by Coronavirus or not.
- The Coronavirus got spread by animals and the reason starts from Wuhan.
- Corona also means the 'sides of the sun'; crown.
- All the 6 Coronas have been studied and vaccines have been found for them early.
- 10 thousand years ago this Corona was affected by mammals and wild birds in China.
- More patients got admitted and the main common similarity among them was, all of them were inside the Wuhan market.
  - → Wuhan Market– A place where wild animals have been captured and killed alive in front of customers.
- No actions were taken by the government towards the Wuhan market.
- Still there is no clue whether it was caused by bats or not, because it came from the bats was the official response.
- As soon as Corona gets affected, the body's immunity gets reduced and affects the throat and respiratory system.

27th January

- The Wuhan major said 'fighting against Covid is like fighting against an invisible villain, don't know about it and even before getting time to study the virus it is getting spread like fire'.
- 3000 got affected and 80 died in China.
- The vaccine may be found in the next three months.
- The virus can be alive in the outer environment for 5 days.
- Both public and private transportation are frozen, as a precaution measure in China.
- People in China stored food for the next one month from the nearest supermarket after waiting in front of the mall; food rates increased drastically.
- Live animal markets are kept closed (Wuhan).
- As per the speculation this virus got out in December mid and started to spread from then on. China had many problems (Hong Kong issue), so they tried to hide this Corona from the outside world. Even after fifteen days, they couldn't suppress this so the Chinese government officially announced it. "Novel CoronaVirus, the new seventh type of Coronavirus is affecting us. From animals to humans and no matter which animal we eat humans will get this

Corona". Then they realised this started from animals, but doubts how from animal to human can be spread.

- 50 lakhs people came and went in Wuhan at New Year time and that's how other countries started showing affected Corona cases.
- Corona came from snakes to humans, snakes that have been eaten from Wuhan; After research, the scientists concluded snakes don't have any Corona and pointed towards bats.
- Corona didn't affect or kill any young people.
- The virus can be alive in the body and only get active after fourteen days.
- No confirmed cases in India, Malaysia, Singapore, Indonesia, America and Australia.
- Still the government and the WHO have no idea from where the Corona got started.
- Corona will be alive in the air for twenty four hours and it's an airborne virus.
- Wuhan has been on lockdown due to excess crowds. If the people are going out of the city then they should be scanned and made sure they don't have the virus. More than ten cities have been locked down in China by now.

28th January

- 4,500 affected 80+ dead in China.
- China started building two new hospitals; one with a thousand beds and the other with two thousand beds.
- 'Eat cooked food and avoid pets' Chinese research team to the people.
- 'Wuhan won't fall, Wuhan will be back' statement by the Chinese government.
- 'No change from the snake, nor from the bats now' Washington Times. "This virus is Wuhan laboratory specimen and it got out accidentally; this virus has been out since November and the government hid it from the world. From December 31 in just 26 days 4500 people got affected. Doesn't make any sense, they need more time and the government hid. 13 cities closed and out of no option they revealed the virus news internationally.
  - → This Wuhan market has been live for more than 100 years and people were eating there as well. So the virus from the market had a lower chance there than in the lab. The virus they created in the lab got out by accident."
  - → Many other media are asking about this to China, and China is not responding to any.

- The Mayor of Wuhan 'puts all the blame on himself and plans to leave China' still doesn't tell the real situation.
- WHO→ 'It happened only in China but not in any other countries so keep calm. The people dead are all from China, almost 105 dead in China but not in other countries.'
- A female employee from Germany went to China to celebrate and reached back. This happened way before the Corona spread. There was no checking at the airport. She started going to the office as well. She and her colleagues went for a meeting and she started to show the symptoms of Covid-19 and the government looked at her in detail and they found out the lady had Corona. Two people in Germany got Corona from her.
- China hid the Corona incident because their stock got down and they stopped because it was hitting the world economy.

29th January

- China (Hong Kong) created a vaccine for Corona and that can't be given to humans.
- 6 thousand got affected and 35 deaths in China.
- All planes going to China have been stopped.
- WHO made a statement that led the people to be there in China itself to avoid spreading and let the people go to their countries after settling down.
    - → The USA and Indian governments said 'no' to that and arranged a plane to bring their citizens back. The Indian government will put the people in quarantine for 14 days and after making sure they are safe only the government will let them go to their houses.
    - → 'No! try to understand!' said WHO to the USA and India for the statement of bringing back their people. *The form that the Indian made had an option 'Do you have any symptoms?'
- Rates for everything increased in China.
- Affected rates and death rates are x5-x6 times higher than the official reports says the common people in China.

30th January

- 7 to 7.5 thousand affected 170 deaths (more than 70 thousand said by common people) in China.
- Covid affected people are trying to spread it in China.
- Many Chinese politicians and doctors took leaves and gave large excuses for them to stay safe from Corona, and the government denied and made them do jobs deliberately.
- All Indians who got trapped in Wuhan have been brought back to India and after 14-28 days of quarantine they are allowed to go to their home.

31st January

- 10 thousand got affected, 200 dead worldwide.
- WHO officially warned everyone to be careful.
- Share market getting down.
- WHO→ don't panic, increase personal hygiene, use hot water more, avoid touching (physical contact), use face masks, and eat more home-cooked foods.
- Total deaths in China is 800 but the death due to Corona is 800 in just Wuhan.
- 2:00 a flight from China to Delhi especially for the students & workers to get back to India. All the 400 students are held in Haryana, Haryana Punjab zone. The Indian army was incharge of their shelter and safety. After spending 28 days and confirming no symptoms they were allowed to go to their houses.
- A girl from China reached Kolkata on 23rd and from there to Kochi/Trivandrum from there to Thrissur. 30th was when she was confirmed Corona positive.
- The Indian government decided to make leave till Feb 16th and they extended till March 1st, Full lockdown.

2nd February

- 24 countries were affected by Corona.
- 300 people recovered, 304 deaths and 14 thousands affected worldwide.
- The 1st person to die outside China was in the Philippines.
- Depression and loneliness started to make people abnormal.
- 850 people were already brought to India and 350 brought yesterday by 'Air India'.
    - → Just because it was a government they arranged and took the Indian's from China.
    - → 'But if 'Air India' was sold to any private sector they wouldn't have done that' internet talks.
- Another positive case in Kerala, total 2 cases in India.

3rd February

- 17 thousand affected and 350 deaths worldwide.
- 650 Indians in Wuhan got collected by 'Air India' plus 7 Maldives students.
- China banned the US because the US stopped all the trades and other countries copied this. 'We need face masks at least provided as that', China is asking other countries.
- Thailand came up with hope by testing a mixed up medicine of 2 medicines and tested on 3 people.
  (1) Recovering.
  (2) Racks stopped giving.
  (3) Still going on.
    → WHO didn't appreciate this because they didn't make a proper lab report or test on any animals before.
- China asking for help from Europe (a rare incident) {Indicates helplessness}.
- 'Jumbo jets' made two trips from New Delhi to Wuhan.
    → Air India operated both times to take the people along with all repair parts and spare parts in case of any repair due to 25 years old.
- 3 cases in Kerala.
- 3 people from China came to Kerala.

9th February

- 37 thousand affected and 800 deaths in China.
- 47% of Corona spread in China happened due to hospital visits.
- One YouTuber in China who spoke about the situation in China got arrested and kept in an isolated area.
- All other countries isolated China, and China is asking for help from the USA.
- World workshop (China) has been shut down for a month now.
- The Apple company asked to open their plants in China, but got rejected by the government.
- Viruses can be alive on the surface for almost 5 days.

➢ Virus-affected people have been going to hospital since December starting, claiming severe headaches, vomiting and throat pain. And a doctor, Dr Li Wenliang, takes blood samples and tests and research and comes to a conclusion that this is a new virus, more severe than SARS and he posted on social media and shared it with other government officials.

➢ And the government arrested him saying he is anti-Chinese and made him sign the papers saying 'he is a bad doctor, he will never spread fear mongers among people, never lies, and will do his job properly.'

➢ After the government announces the Corona things, the people made the doctor to be released and made him go free.

➢ The doctor started treating the people again in the same hospital and got hit by Corona, they isolated him and he died due to Corona in that same hospital.

➢ After his death '#freedom of speech' trended on Chinese social media and the government removed the posts regarding this in just after a few hours.[1]

• The journalist who spread the video and reports of the real Corona thing got tracked on social media and removed her posts and warned her to 'shut up' by the Chinese authorities.

• Petrol, diesel rate reduced.

• WHO warned China that 'the Corona pandemic may get higher in the future'.

---

[1] *Explained properly in 'Anoroc- Duo'*

14th February

- 1.5 thousand dead, 65+ affected rates in China.
- China asked for help directly to WHO and WHO research terms entered in. WHO then comes to the conclusion that 'China's testing methods are not proper. Instead of taking samples, giving it to the lab→ The people with doubts are also checking, by which the person will spread to 100 others, making the people who came to check due to doubt go home with confirmed virus in them. Instead of making those people who came to check doubt and return them with Corona. Make a system in which you can identify the affected people instantly. And they used the proper method'.
- The forced Covid testing by the government is how the Covid is spreading in China.
- The Corona scene still lasts the summer and may extend even more in China.
- China's economy is drowning.
- People in China started to think China will become a democratic country because of Lee Jeing's attitude and white-collar shittery towards handling the Corona situation in Wuhan.
- Singapore's prime minister, 'Singapore's economy will get resuscitated because of a

lack of products being imported from China'.

- Near Cambodia, a ship has been stopped which has been in the sea for more than 2 months; Almost all countries, Japan, Malaysia, Singapore, and China have already claimed 'No ship has to be halted in our port' as a precaution because the chances of the Corona spreading is higher, Corona and other diseases are higher in ships. And the ship halted in Cambodia, the Cambodian government approved the request from the ship and tested every person in the ship in port and confirmed no Covid victims.
- Pulwama, Jammu and Kashmir was attacked in 2019 and 40 Indian soldiers died on this valentine's day.

21st February

- The recovery rate in China increased from 1% to 10%, and 6% of people recovered from Corona in Wuhan city.
- 75 thousand affected overall, 2,236 deaths in China.
- In Japan, 600 people were affected. One person had Corona in a ship so if the person gets out it may cause like in China; so the government decided not to let anyone out of the ship, leading it to affect all the passengers on the ship. In the ship itself.
- China people slightly lean toward traditional medicines.
- Jail in China discovered 500 people affected by Corona, and 20 officers were dismissed.
- No Corona case in North Korea.
- Kim blocked every contact with China.
- In South Korea 800 people were affected by an old lady who was a member of an ashram cult. It spread to 800 people in just 36 hrs.
- Corona was affected.
  *China is the highest.
  *South Korea 800.
  *Japan 600 but in the middle of the sea (ship).
- Test vaccines will be out in the month of April, said a few organisations.

∇   'If we increase the immunity in our body we can fight against Corona' -talk among doctors.

2nd March

- The stock market rucked.
- The Iran Minister said they have reduced Corona all over Iran and after the press, he died.
- Two more cases in India: Telangana, North India people who came from (Iry and Kuwait).
- 2 people in America died due to Corona today.
- All countries lied about Corona being controlled. Because their economy crashes, if the economy crashes the other countries won't trade with them.
- 'The vaccine will be available in just 18 months' -official statement by the WHO.
- 53 countries are affected by Corona so far.
- The South Korean president bowed his head as an apology to the people because of the carelessness of the lady who spread it. The people are shouting to give the death sentence for that lady's carelessness, 'increase the punishment can reduce the carelessness.'
- 3 thousand dead worldwide.
- Developed countries are fucked right now.
- Organisations for economic cooperation development announced that Corona will be the villain to crash the world economy.

5th March

- Affected rates 1 lakh and 3 thousand dead worldwide; 80 thousand in China.
- 30 people in India, from that 15 were Italians.
- 80% of people recovered in China by boosting their immunity.
- Italy, Iran, South Korea→ more than 1 thousand affected.
- Switzerland→ a 74 year-old lady got affected.
- Share market crashing.
- Corona will spread more, humans are the biggest enemy of humans. After that comes the virus we should not panic but we need to fight against it, said Dr Liptin virologists in America. (Yesterday).
- Italy to Delhi went to a birthday party and the guy was found positive and all the students from there were from 2 schools and the school gave leave to entire students as a precaution.
- People from Italy showed negative first and positive later (after 15 days).
- Global searching will be put to buy the health minister.
- Chinese people who visited back to China brought Corona along with them. So the government made a rule, 'whoever gets back

to China they need to go under quarantine for 20 days'.

- People from Iran, North Korea, China, and Italy need to show the certificate claiming they didn't have Corona from March 10 while travelling.
- 20 seconds hand wash, no touching eyes, nose, mouth, avoid social crowds, 6 feet distance, personal hygiene$\Rightarrow$ WHO's guide line.
- Benjamin Netanyahu went to Israel and greeted Namaste as the Coronavirus scare spread.
- Delhi school leave for next 3-4 days. Middle East (Indigo flight) for a meeting and he made contact with 80 people to quarantine and in that 34 people are showing little inclination of having Corona.
- Modi and Amit Shah skipped Holi Milan due to Corona.

13th March

- ∇ WHO officially announced Corona as a global pandemic.
- Major shops and offices are closed worldwide due to fear of Corona.
- The majority of the people who got affected are recovering (more than 80%) and people who had incurable diseases had died 5% worldwide.
- The Canadian President's wife has tested Covid positive today.
- Started using Namaste worldwide, Trump and UK princes' videos became viral.
- From the start - till of the spread of Corona worldwide,
  * China- 80,815.
  * Italy- 15,113.
  * Iran- 11k.
  * South Korea- 8k.
  * Spain- 4k.
  * Germany- 3k.
  * France- 2k.
  * US- 1,800.
  * Switzerland- 1,100.
  * India- 81.
- New Corona in decreasing order of the spreading, Iran→ Spain→ Germany→ Switzerland→ US→ Denmark→ South Korea→ Norway→ Austria.

- 1,28,274 affected, 5082 dead and 70,719 recovered in India.
- India's first death due to Corona happened in Karnataka→ 76 year person who came from the Middle East.
- The IPL has been postponed to April.
- Schools, offices, malls, and theatres have been closed in North Indian states.
- An IT guy got married in February and went to Greece for a honeymoon, from there he got affected by Corona, no symptoms showed at that time and after a few days, it got confirmed. All those who contacted him got quarantined.
- A guy from Qatar came to India because his father was ill and he got affected by Corona and was admitted to the same hospital as his father was hospitalised. He did a video call with his dad and even after his dad's death he didn't go to the funeral because people around him may get affected by Corona because of him.

16th March

- In 140 countries more than 1 lakh 60 thousand people got affected, more than 75% recovered 6500 deaths worldwide.
- Cases in India- 119.
  * Maharashtra- 37.
  * Kerala- 24 in that 12 are active.
  * Tamil Nadu- 1.
- Tamil Nadu has announced that schools, colleges, and theatres should be closed till March 31st.
- The Indian government made a strict rule towards shopkeepers 'if the price for the things are raised then the government will take strict action.'

20th March

- Worldwide confirmed cases→ 245818 and deaths→ 1047.
- The Chinese government went to the doctor's house who warned about the Corona and apologised to his family for not taking the doctores words seriously. Ths doctor died due to Corona.
- In India, the confirmed cases are 186 cases.
- Modi announced, 'on March 22 from 7am to 9pm no one should go out but instead stay in the house as a lockdown as a practice for upcoming days.'

22nd March

- 3 lakh affected 13 thousand dead 96 thousand recovered worldwide.
- China→ 81 thousand total reported cases and no cases from Wuhan for a week.
  *Affected rates.
    - → Italy 53 thousand.
    - → Spain 28 thousand.
    - → US 26 thousand.
- 328 affected in the whole of India.
  * Kerala 49.
  * Andhra Pradesh 3.
  * Telangana 21.
  * Karnataka 19.
  * Tamil Nadu 6.
    - → A necessary state will be opened.
    - → Date boards are closed entirely.
    - → The interstate bus will be almost nil.
    - → Till March 31 ban for trains except for goods.
- 75 districts should be locked down until the 31st of March.
- Actress Kaneka Kapoor spread Corona from the U.K to all the way to India.
- International flights will not be landing for the next 1 week, domestic flights will be reduced.

29th March

- 6 lakh are affected and 30 thousand dead worldwide; India→1,000 cases.
- India faced a lack of testing kits (1 kit rate = around 4,500 rs) time took for the result was ten hours to one day to test the sample and these are imported.
- Minal Bhosale, a 31-year-old lady in India, founded a new testing kit{complicated 8 months pregnant}.[2]
    - → In 6 weeks she completes and submits for approval and on the next day she is admitted to the hospital for a caesarean (delivery) and gives birth to a female child. The test can be done in two hours and for one kit it costs 1,400rs.
- Narendra Modi apologises to all citizens for the 21 days of lockdown hardships.

---

[2] *Explained properly in 'Anoroc- Duo'*

30th March

- In more than half of the developed countries the governments requested for 'stay home'.
- 'China is back to normal'→ Wall Street Journal.
- On 23rd Jan 2am in China Wuhan provinces announced a lockdown and it was done from 10 am.
    - → Road to Road lockdown (Road-block).
    - → School, college, work lockdown (Smart classes/online classes and work from home).
    - → Body temperature became strict while entering or exiting the apartment compound.
    - → The Chinese government introduced military precautions.
    - → Created plastic walls on areas and apartments to reduce the virus spread.
    - → Once in 2 days 1 person in a family can go out and collect food and necessary things in a alloted isolated time. And a limited amount of the supplies were sold per person, not to store for more days, to prevent the shortage of the goods. And no extra price.

> → The entire China is under CCTV surveillance to check who all are not taking the lockdown seriously.
> → Phone numbers tracked facial recognition systems in CCTV to identify which citizens had been out without taking the rules seriously and they revived calls from the government.
> → The safe distance is a rule and if the people break the rule→ then directly to the jail.

- Italy, Spain, and Canada have fine systems when the rule is broken.
- International flights have been banned.
- Donald Trump said planning for a lockdown and the government rejected his suggestion.
- Many other countries are planning for a lockdown.
- Migrant workers in Delhi, Africa, and Thailand are facing problems even in Italy.
- North Korea with no Corona cases, even from the past also they were safe.
- North Korea is also following all the prevention steps followed by China.

31st March

- Worldwide 2.5 lakh affected and 1,047 death rates.
- Italian people are getting affected more than that of China.
- 'Due to strict lockdown, China is free from Corona' as per the media.
- Modi announced that from 7 am to 9 pm people should sit at home, no matter what. At 5 pm make a clap or make a sound with the plate to appreciate the workers who helped in the safety of the people, police officers, hospital staff etc etc.
    → Work from home should be imprinted.
    → Offices to be sanitised.
- 186 confirmed cases in India.
    → One guy out of 3 in Tamil Nadu recovered.
    → 25 active cases in Kerala.
    → No need to fear for food, the government will provide all needs for food to the people.

∇ The Chinese government apologised to the doctor who informed about the Corona at the initial stage. The government authorities went to their houses and apologised to the family members, those doctors died due to Corona.[3]

---

[3] *Explained properly in 'Anoroc- Duo'*

7th April

- America was the last to establish lockdown and they have the highest death rate now.
- India entered the 2nd week of lockdown in the whole of 3 weeks.
  - Some state chief ministers want to extend the lockdown, but others don't agree.
- The prime minister and the chief minister had a video conference.
- Telangana chief ministers need to extend the lockdown.
- Punjab- If we didn't harvest at this time then there will be a shortage of food in the whole state and in the nation as well.

9th April

- 3 lakh people recovered from Corona worldwide.
- WHO didn't confirm the positive role of hydroxychloroquine yet.
- China officially announced they will also donate to countries and instead of donating they took the order and made the payment and sent back the rest of unused donation received PPE's at the initial stage. And it caused problems. In many countries, few of the products are damaged on a large scale and in Norway, Netherland and Spain they returned those back to China and China defended itself by claiming they didn't know to read the manual inside it.
- Trump in the press meeting said, 'we ordered and paid for it after that only they banned it, so China will give and if they don't then they will face problems from us'.

- Last week, more than 30 countries' prime ministers called Modi and asked for help with hydroxychloroquine.[4]
- India has increased the production capacity of hydroxychloroquine and is willing to provide to other countries as well.

---

[4] *Explained properly in 'Anoroc- Duo'*

- India banned China due to lack of stuff that was imported from there. Modi and Trump phones China for the issue and Modi tweeted as both countries will live together without talking about the media.
- India delivered to the USA and even claimed that, 'India will be providing to nearby countries and if any other countries need any things we will provide to them.'
- 'India is a great country and thanks to all Indian sisters,' said in a tweet and press in the White House.
- Odissa made a statement to close till June 17th (school and colleges) till April 30 state lockdown.
- Railways planned for 108 trains for good transport and India railway is planning to convert the train to hospital environment if the Corona situation goes out of hand, to overcome the hospital shortage⇒ Government public transport, not the private sector.

12th April

- China is trying to buy many companies all around the world, especially with countries that haven't done any trade with China so far.
- Japan comments 'Companies in China have been locked in, full of pity, if they went to work you can come and work in Japan' this statement made Chinese people angry and officially made discomfort regarding their comment afterward.

26th April

- The 1st case was reported in January; from China to South Korea.
    - The patient was a 31-year-old female who went to a big church and she spread.
    - The government will not disclose her identity for her safety reasons.
    - From 30 people it reached 1000 cases in February.

1st May

- The US started accepting new applications from India. "We made the final decision to move the business from China and look to improve business in India" -Pompeo.
- ∇ Trump at a press conference.
    Reporter: "Do you believe that China made the virus and kept it out of the lab?"
    Trump: "Yes, from the lab,"
    Reporter: "From that lab? Do you have proof or evidence to justify?"
    Trump: "Yes, I've strong evidence,"
    Reporter: "What is the evidence,"
    Trump: "Sorry, I can't disclose that!"
- ∇ Wuhan institution of virology has been active for 45 years; when it was upgraded for the research and other works Americans contributed a lot of money, along with France 'Especially focusing on bats based viruses' SARS was first to be identified and recognised by the Wuhan institution of virology.
- The European head made a strong voice asking the investigation team "How did it all start in China?"
- WHO is also expecting China to invite us in to investigate the virus and we are ready in making the term for that.

- The Wuhan institution stated that, 'it didn't break from the virology lab nor did they spread it internationally or they started the Corona,' China said.
- American point of view→ 'It got out from Wuhan lab accidentally (as per their intelligence report)'.
- NIA→ This Corona has nothing to do with humans, humans don't make this but Trump says China made it deliberately for some reason.

2nd May

- Japan news says 'Kim Jong Un' is dead.
- South Korea- no problem with Kim Jong Un.
- Kim Jong Un went to an inauguration (Fertiliser factory plant) after twenty days of missing.
  - → April 10th was the last time he was seen in the media.
- Still no Corona cases from North Korea.
- South Korea news, 'Kim was having social distance due to Corona and that's why he was missing.'
- China is the one that provided more PPE and ventilator to India. That's why India is not putting any investigation acquisition to China like, USA, Australia, or Germany.
- Even after Corona, China is one who is going to give a push to India to raise the India economy.
- The WHO chairman election in Japan is 2020.

3rd May

- In Taiwan→ 600 people were affected and 10 died.
- Taiwan fully supports the creation of vaccines and is ready to help scientists to discover the vaccine and they are not concerned about the patent.
- North Korea shot at the South Korean border for no particular reason and South Korea killed 40 people in return (Border shooting).{North Korea trying to show off}.
- On 31st December a guy from China went to Taiwan (affected person) that's how Taiwan got the virus.
- After China the 2nd case was in Taiwan.
- After realising the unknown and dangerous virus the government stopped everyone from Wuhan to Taiwan.
- First to stop passengers from China was Taiwan. Taiwan understood it could be passed from human to human and announced the world, but no country gave any type of concern, WHO ignored Taiwan.
- Taiwan started to manufacture PPE.
    - → India, Italy, and France are asking from them.
- Baseball matches were not discontinued but they kept robots instead of humans.
- Taiwan is ready to help with vaccines. They announced worldwide that, 'we are ready to

share our research papers and willing to give their scientists to work on the vaccine with other countries. Share your research work with us or we will work together and find the vaccine and we don't want any money.'

- No closing medical public gatherings areas in Taiwan.
- Taiwan sent 1 million medical equipment to other countries.
- The US tweeted that Taiwan needs to be added as a United Nations, WHO member because they are helping other countries. And China publicly offended the US claiming 'you are interfering in our own national problems'.

∇ Taiwan was a beast at that time.

8th May

- 'Patient Zero' details asked by the USA secretary of state, Mike Pompeo. The Chinese haven't revealed that yet.
- 57 years old female 'Vay' from South China was patient zero as per Wall Street journal.
- 'Pangolins and human Corona have the highest match,' -China's statement.
- 'Vay' used to sell shrimps and she used the public toilet in Wuhan market, and the toilet was less hygienic and due to that Coronavirus affected her' was her statement, must have spread by the toilet. Or must have affected the people and was mutating to get strong and when it got stronger it hit the health of the human it showed up.
- → 'Vay' got fewer and went to the nearest hospital, got pills and went back. After 14 days she wasn't able to walk. She was diagnosed and admitted in the hospital and after her admission, the people near her shop got health problems and thus the hospital found the virus and the market has some kind of connection→ the hospital informs to higher authorities→ the authorities made the doctor (Dr Li Wenliang) write an apology letter for spreading the virus. It spread without checking and it reached the maximum in January and the market is closed.

- The unhygienic toilet in Wuhan was the head of the news.
- 'Vay' had 10 thousand dollars for the treatment and after one month of treatment, she got back to life. Her daughter also got affected in mid-January and now they both are safe.
- Wuhan wet market was closed on Jan 1st and the market opened in April.
- Criticism on the international level and China 'didn't give a fuck' attitude.
- H1B visa→ no one from outside India to get the job until and unless the majority of India got back for next 1-1 1⁄2 years.
- Donald Trump's P.A tested Covid positive and Trump is being Covid tested on a daily basis for the next 15 days.

24th May

- China's government told their labs to destroy Coronavirus samples to reduce the biosafety risk.
- Pompeo says 'evidence shows that Coronavirus emerged from a China lab.'
- America claims the Corona came from a Chinese lab and Trump made an official statement saying he saw the evidence to prove that his statement is right in a press conference. He said a week early that aired yesterday and the main virologist said that 'We had 3, not 1 Coronavirus with us' said the Pompeo's scientist.
- SARS was brought by bats and SARS comes under Corona family, so studying what all viruses does the bat have kept few bats for that research; they got 3 Coronaviruses excluding the Covid-19. We get the current Corona samples only on December 31st. When we tested this Covid-19 we also had no idea about the virus so we weren't able to figure it out at that time.
- China tells the US to stop wasting time in the Corona battle (warned officially).
- Taiwan- China problem and India put nose in their problem.

3rd July

- More than 100 countries are interested in funding for the Corona vaccine.

- Co-vaxin, Bharat biotech. 7 vaccines were working, but co-vaxin was done after the first preclinical test passed.
  - → Phase 1→ 250 people.
  - → Phase 2→ 750 volunteers who haven't been affected by Covid-19, age group from 12-65.
- The companies haven't fixed the rate of vaccines but will be easily available to all Indians.
- Modi went to Ladakh, near the border attacked area (250 km away) and gave a motivational speech to the soldiers.
- ∇ 70 people who got injured in the India-China attack were visited by Modi.

9th August

- Russian vaccine (Gamaleya research institution x Defense ministry).
- America is going to ban all Chinese products Vivo, Oppo, and also planning to stop partnerships with China, not at all TikTok.
- Corona spikes are introduced to a common cold virus and injected in the vaccine.
- Canada and the United Kingdom government→ Russian hackers are trying to hack us and steal our vaccine formula and we are 95% sure about that.
- India's oxford 3rd trial vaccine got approved and is going to be tested on 1700 people.
- Russia did the 3 tests in less than 70 people and had fewer (<10) and 32 in the 3rd stage. August 12 register. September→ mass production. October→ available to common people.

→ Ambani 4th richest man (80 billion).
→ Mark Zuckerberg is the 3rd richest man.
→ Bill Gates is the 2nd richest.
→ Jeff Bezos 1st.

11th August

- Russia is the first to come up with the vaccine→ Sputnik V.
- Putin tested the vaccine in one of his daughters.
- Russia only completed 2 phases of the research and they started the production, manufacturing, launch and from September the Russian government will provide vaccines to all their citizens.
- Russia is not going to force anyone to take the vaccine, only to the volunteers.
- 1 billion orders have been inquired to Russia by 20 countries and India is one among them.
- WHO claimed Russia has to test the vaccine for approval to the health benefits of the people. And Russia replied 'Other countries don't like Russia being known as a powerful country, just a western propaganda.'
- America and UK vaccines are in the development stage three.
- ∇ Covid-19 patients in Tamil Nadu, India are promoting and supporting *Siddha* medicine as it cured many Corona cases.

13th August

- Russian government started putting terms and conditions for vaccine,
  - → 1) The vaccine is not made for everyone and not everyone should do it.
  - → 2) Only for the 16-60 age group.
  - → Russian doctors→ We have done the test on people from 16-60 and with just 70 participants. Will start the research soon.
- China has a weird fact that, if a Chinese company is working outside China, then that country should need to give their data to China. And TikTok was stealing data from people using it, so India banned TikTok along with America.
- America was planning to buy TikTok and sell it as 'TikTok America'.
- 3 billion US dollars before lockdown and 5 billion now, Ambani planning to buy TikTok→ TikTok Indian.
- → America, Britain, Canada received more than a thousand courier packages with normal seeds in them, to make a review of the courier that the company had sent.

18th August

- In May, a beach in Wuhan conducted a swimming pool party without the masks, no social distance and other Covid precaution measures kit, a post-lockdown party. 15 thousand people attended and the party had a 'couple discounts' on tickets.
- Trump→ 'all those American companies which are in China, come back and they will get a reduction on taxes.'
- America stopped giving contracts to companies that are linked with China.

14th September

- Dr. Li-Meng Yan, a virologist from Hong Kong, announced she will be publishing a scientific paper regarding Corona any time soon. And her statement towards the **Corona** were:-
  - → 1) Corona is a man-made virus, made in a military-controlled lab in China; artificially made, not formed from bats or any other animals.
  - → 2) Corona will spread from human to human. It was known by the government from December itself because 'we' are the term who informed them, but they turned it down and tried to suppress us.
  - → The main reason Corona spread in China⇒ allowed people to travel everywhere.
  - → 3) I've proof for all these, there are a few things to check for viruses by which we can say that this virus is man-made and not formed naturally and I've researched it.[5]
- ❖ At the time of December mid 'a virus has been affected in Wuhan' a news they got in Hong Kong university.

---

[5] *Explained properly in 'Anoroc- Duo'*

❖ The head of the virology department sends Dr. Li-Meng Yan to go to Wuhan and study what's going on because she was well knowledgeable in the field and she also knew Mandarin language.

❖ She goes to the market, doctors, patients and studies the virus. At the start of 2020 the Chinese government stopped their research quickly and sent her back to Hong Kong and after the virus started to spread intensely the government allowed them to continue the research. After a 2 week break, from January she started her research and found this is a human-to-human virus.

❖ At New year's time, Dr. Li-Meng Yan altered everyone regarding the virus but none gave a fuck; she went to CDC (Center for Disease Control) and even alerts WHO in January starting, which informed Chinese authorities. She even informs many department heads. And the reply she got was→ 'stay away from this or else you will disappear.'

❖ After that she contacted a Chinese YouTube and with his help she eloped from China to America with all her proofs, research paper and documents. The YouTuber started to talk about the Coronavirus thing via media and in February they admitted a virus outbreak had happened, because of the media or else still the Chinese government wouldn't have informed this out.

- Western media didn't take 'Dr Li-Meng Yan' whistleblowing seriously.
- ▽ 'JC45' and 'dxc21' are the combinations of Corona.
- ▽ Dr. Li Meng Yan⇒ 'as a whistleblower I can't say where I am but I'll publish the scientific papers soon'.
- She strongly says China's military developed the Corona.
- In the India-China border they diploid Fibre cables, internet, and phone facilities are all installed→ indications of long-term war somewhere in future.

3rd November

- China- 100 cases.
- The United Kingdom is under lockdown.
- In Germany, cases are increasing rapidly.
- Chinese vaccine ⇒ being brought to the Middle East to reach people.
- Russian vaccine ⇒ Sputnik V started to be used in people above 60 years of age.
- In February WHO team went to China to find out the Corona starting and China initially didn't show where it started and deviated them and when the team was searching by themselves China's head term spoke with the WHO head and covered. China initially covered the origin of Corona. When they didn't give a proper transparent report to the community, the united communist nation announced they will be going and finding the origin -New York times.
- ❖ Still, the origin of the Corona is a mystery like the Spanish flu.
- Brazil is having an anti-vaccine protest.
- India negotiated that 1 in 2 people should get the vaccine as a deal to manufacture the vaccine in India.
- Delhi- 6 thousand people affected in just 24 hours.
- Delhi and Kerala are facing the worst in the 2nd wave.

21st December

- Boris Johnson announced a strict lockdown on London on Christmas, yesterday.
- South Africa also got mutated Coronavirus→ higher effectiveness than the 1st wave.
- 7 crore 72 lakh people got affected and 17 lakh died worldwide.
- The second wave of Corona started September mid but it was a mutated version.
- The United Kingdom and South Africa mutated Corona are different when compared to one another.
- ∇ "Does the vaccine work on Corona?" a question of concern in the media and internet.
- US experts ⇒ May be less effective at first but still, it works. (Just a theory by them).
- WHO⇒ Every virus will mutate. That's not a new thing→ but we need some time to study this.
- Maharashtra, India is having night lockdown.
- India stopped flights from the United Kingdom and made all UK flights passengers quarantined.

22nd December

- WHO says the United Kingdom is safe from Corona and the United Kingdom claims that they are not at all safe from the newly mutated variant.
- 40 countries stopped transport to and fro from the United Kingdom.
- Israel and China are under strict lockdown and prevented flight transport.
- Biden and Israel's president took the vaccine.
- The United Kingdom is planning to lockdown till everyone gets vaccinated.
- People who got affected by Corona has the immunity a little lower and these people are getting affected by black fungus, Delhi and Gujarat peoples 50% we can physically see the fungus.

23rd December

- 3 days back a new strand of Corona has been discovered in the UK and 50 countries have stopped all the flights from the UK; travel ban.
- They found the new variant in a village in the UK and the next day in London and on December 1st 1000 people were affected by that in London.
- Maharashtra and Karnataka, in India are having night lockdowns.

24th December

- United Kingdom→ Identifies 2 types of Corona in September mid not the killing type but the spreading type.
    - → December 1 more than 1,000 people got affected. Spreading in children's as well.
- South Africa discovered a third type Corona, (more powerful than elsewhere).
- An international ban on South Africa and the United Kingdom and the United Kingdom got the 3rd type of Corona.
- The United Kingdom and South Africa are the countries that are researching Corona and that's why they found it.
- 40 thousand Corona cases in the United Kingdom today. So they introduced zone type lockdown (4 types in total).
- The United Kingdom research term found out the new Corona variant because we were researching it day in and day out. "Every country should do the research to find out if there are any new Corona roaming in their country." -UK research terms official statement.
- No confirmation of both the new types of Corona in India 1 thousand people came from the United Kingdom 14 days ago and they are not Corona affected.

- 22 people were identified to be Corona positive but their RNA is sent to a lab and the result will be reached the day after tomorrow.

2021

62

2nd January

- 60 thousand cases in the UK, more cases than the first wave.
- New Covid cases strain 1st wave in U.K.
- U.K→ at least 1st dose of the vaccine should be accessible to the citizens. (10 million vaccines should be brought).
- Fizer 95% efficiency needed to be transported in a sub-zero temperature.
- All health officials claim the new vaccine from the UK can also be declined with the current vaccine.
- In first half of 2021, 30 crore people should be vaccinated (not decided whether just the 1st dose to the people or both first and second doses to as people as possible or vise-versa).
- Front line workers (doctor, lawyer, public works) gave 2 crore vaccines to them.
- 'New Covid case, strain: 4, more test positive in India, total case reached 29'- says the Indian government.
- Puni based company created covi-sheild vaccine to be given to the citizens (India).
  - → 70% efficiency.

4th January

- 'Corona vaccine may not work in South African strain' -UK scientists.
- The South African Corona variant is dangerous compared to other mutated variants.
- The South African Corona variant hasn't entered India yet.
- UK variants are spreading so fast.
- 'Jack Ma is missing from October' - Business today.
- Bird flu confirmed in over 1,700 migrated birds found dead in Himachal Pradesh.
- 'Alappuzha, Kottayam in Kerala is on high alert after Bird flu cases detected' - Hindustan times.
- The H5N8 virus will affect only birds due to this the Kerala government killed over 48 thousand birds and the government is willing to pay compensation to the farms.

6th January

- Congo, Africa→ a girl gets fewer, the family goes to the nearest hospital thinking they have Corona and they do the test, but the result shows Corona negative. The doctors checked for Ebola and that also showed negative. After this the doctor freaks out thinking the family has 'Disease- X'; that was warned 2 years ago by the WHO. Which was stated to be the century's worst disease.
    - Disease-X→ spreads faster than Covid and kills faster than Ebola.
    - 'Doctors who helped discover Ebola warn of a new fatal infection called Disease-X' -First post.
- ▽ Disease-X is zoonotic disease, the disease spreads because of deforestation. As the forest gets lower as humans conquer, the disease gets to humans and from there it will spread from human to human.

16th February

- 5 people tested with the South African variant; Brazil variant (P1).
    - → 4 tourists from Japan went to the Amazon forest this year, and they went back to Japan after exploring the forest. When they are Covid tested the Japan government officially announced that the people are having Corona but couldn't recognise which type and suggested it to be a new type of Corona (Not sound anywhere so far). So places check the area about the new variant- '12 mutations had happened in this variant' -says the Japan government.
- Spreading like a wildfire in Brazil and the government is not willing to put a national lockdown yet.
    - → Just after this the Corona hike in Brazil has reached a situation where people are not able to go to hospital because of hospital facility shortage (oxygen cylinders, medicines and other necessary facilities).
- Maharashtra and Kerala are the only states in India having the largest Corona cases.
- India is controlling the Corona very impressively even though it is one of the most populated countries.

→ 1 in every 5 people got affected by Corona got immunity against Coronavirus.

23rd February

- Worldwide the Corona cases are getting lower.
- Maharashtra has implied a one week lockdown in Amravati from 22nd Feb till March 1.
- '240 Covid variants are roaming in India'- says the Indian government.

1st March

- Modi took the vaccine today.
- 250rs for vaccines in private hospitals.
- Kerala and Maharashtra are the 2 states testing **Corona** nowadays in whole India and that's why these states are showing highest **Corona** affected rates.

11th March

- Brazil is turning out to be the next Wuhan.
- Brazil last week 4,75,503 new cases.
- 11,009 people died in Brazil.
- P1 variant can be affected to people who are affected by Corona once.
- Brazil had become the breeding ground of Corona.
- 'Nagpur lockdown from March 25-21, likely in more parts of Maharashtra.' NDTV.
- Maharastra turing to be the Indian version of Wuhan.

17th March

- 3k people die each day in Brazil and the government is not allowing lockdowns or telling people to take vaccines.
- 30k cases reported in India.
    - → 945 cases in Tamil Nadu (Less in whole India).
        1. Last few days in India more than 70 districts are having 150% Corona cases.
        2. In the first wave all capital places were facing Covid cases and if the second wave gets in villages or to towns the cases will be drastic.
        3. Testing is getting lower, above 70% of districts having less vaccination and less testing facility.
        4. India is having Corona vaccine wastage (total of 10%)→ UP, Andra, Telangana.
        5. Covid should be prevented from going to small towns.
        6. Currently no full lockdown at the moment but will have micro lockdowns.
        7. No elections are going to be postponed due to Corona.

8. The Karnataka government is providing campus in apartments and in old homes for people who weren't going out.

18th March

- 400 UK, Brazil, South African virus variants.
- First baby in the US born with antibody agents Covid-19.
- 35,871 cases in just one single day in India.
    - → 23k affected cases reported in Maharashtra in the last 24 hrs.
- 158 cases in India in two weeks.
- Death rates decreased a lot (172 in India today).

19th March

- 39,726 cases in India.
    - → Maharashtra had the highest Corona cases so far that too in second wave 25,833.
- Lockdown in Punjab till March 31st. And the government made the terms and conditions.
    1. No colleges or school till March 31.
    2. No offices are allowed and a shift system.
    3. 20 people are allowed to be in social gatherings.
    4. 100 people are allowed to be in the mall or else the shop will be closed.
    5. Theaters to be 50% people.
    6. Sunday full lockdown only essentials services are available.
    7. Saturday 11-12 pm no vehicles on the road for one hour.
    8. Night full curfew (9pm-5am).
    9. No more than 10 guests in the house.
    10. More strictly full lockdown if the precaution didn't lower the Covid cases.
- Cases are high in Germany.
    - → The Brazilian president says 'no' to vaccination.
    - → Total death rates in Brazil are 45k.

22nd March

- Highest Corona cases in Brazil in the whole world.
    - → Brazil so far haven't gone under any lockdown.
    - → Doctors say the second wave is getting higher than the first wave.
    - → The president didn't give much concern or importance to Corona, so that state officials made their own precaution measures, (mask mandatory, social distance). But the president didn't support any of the precautions.
- Totally 20 crore people, 90k people getting affected daily.
- 46,908 reported cases in India.
    - → 1200 plus cases in just Tamil Nadu.
- 12 crore vaccination order and rate is rs180.

25th March

- 53 cases reported in India; highest in 2021 and highest in the past 150 days.
    - → Maharashtra→ 31k cases.
    - → Tamil Nadu→ 1,636 cases.
- Outsiders can only get into Banglore after being tested as Covid -ve.
- SBI reports→ a second wave will be active from 160 days; around May last and the peak Corona will be in April mid. And the lockdowns are not effective.

30th March

- Nagpur hospital admitted 2-3 people on a bed due to lack of facilities.
- 'Covid situation is getting worse' -NDTV.
    - → 56,211 reported in India.
    - → 70k% reported in the US.
    - → 1 lakh cases are increasing in Brazil.
    - → Positivity rates in Maharashtra 23.4%.
    - → Tamil Nadu 2.5%.
- India 5.65% average positive rate.
- 30-40k reported cases in Maharashtra.
    - → Government officials:- get ready for a lockdown' but the people are not willing to.
    - → Lesser chances of getting lockdown in India.

3rd April

- 89129 reported cases in India.
    - → Maharashtra has the highest case 50k.

7th April

- 1,15,269→ reported cases in India in the last 24 hours.
- 20 cities in Gujarat are having night lockdowns.

14th April

- 1.8 lakh affected rate in India in just one day.
    - → More than 7 lakh in Tamil Nadu.
    - → Maharashtra lockdown from today.
- 'Madhya Pradesh hiding Covid death rates.' -NDTV.

19th April

- Stock market going down.
- The highest of all time passed in 24 hrs→ 2,73,810 death cases in India.
- Manmohan Singh was found to be Covid positive.
- Delhi, Maharashtra under lockdown.
- Tamil Nadu having night curfew.
- Highest rates in India are in Maharashtra, Kerala, Karnataka, Tamil Nadu, and Andhra Pradesh.
- From May 1st everyone above 18 years old needs to take the Covid vaccine.

21st April

- 1,82,000 Covid deaths in India; 2 thousand in just past 24 hrs.
- 2 lakh 95 thousand affected rate in India in the last 24 hrs. Maharashtra, Delhi, West Bengal are having the highest.
- West Bengal is having an election and no one gives a concern about the Corona, and no lockdowns as well from the government side.

28th April

- 3,60,960- reported cases in India in the last 24 hrs.
  - → 3,293- deaths in the last 24 hrs.
- Covid-19 lockdown might be imposed in 150 districts with a positivity rate of over 15%.
- CNN, BBC, New York Times- India is having under reporting and the real rates are more than twice-thrice.
- 'Indian Covid deaths toll tops 2,00,000 amid under -reporting claims.' -AXIOS.
- India facing vaccine shortage.
- Tamil Nadu 16k cases reported, 90+ deaths in the last 24 hrs.
  - → In Just Chennai- 4,764 reported cases.
- Covid positive rate in India 20.3%.
- 'Vaccine Hoarding may backfire on nations as India surge threatens world' -NDTV.
- Highest cases reported in India→ Maharashtra, Kerala, Karnataka, UtterPradesh, Tamil Nadu.
- In Delhi 50 new spots have been made as cremation land. The previous cremation lands are full so the people made the parking lots as cremation land.
- Cities began to see an exodus of migrants.

30th April

- 'US tells citizens to leave India as Covid crisis Deepens' -Bloomberg.
- 3.86 lakh Corona cases in 24 hrs in India.
- 3,498 dead rates in India.
  - Tamil Nadu- 17,897 reported.
- Mumbai positivity ratio reduced to 10% from 30%.
- Andes Pradesh chief minister Jagan Mohan Reddy is the one to tell the vaccine shortage publicly.

  $\rightarrow$ September we will give the vaccine to 18-45 aged people. 60 crore vaccines needed to vaccinate this age group. And right now India is producing 7 crore vaccines in a month and that's the highest in the world.
- 'Remdesivir' has been shown as a cure towards Corona and a doctor in Chennai was selling this medicine for 20k, he tried to do business and he got arrested due to that.
- Around 1 million testing kits and ventilators from the US. China is also trying to help. Pakistan claims to help India in this situation. Globally India is seen as a concern.
- West Bengal is under partial lockdown. And there was an election yesterday.
- ❖ Why was the election held in the middle of Corona issues?

1st May

- Globally India has become the highest Corona affected country.
- 40,01,993 reported cases in the last 24 hrs in India.
    - → 3,523 death rates.
    - → Tamil Nadu 18,693 Covid positive, 113 deaths.
- Today at midnight (1am) 10 patients in Gujarath died in the ICU due to a short circuit.
- ❖ 'Shutdown country for weeks, build makeshift hospitals like China.' Dr Fauci on India's Covid crisis.

3rd May

- 'India Covid; Delhi hospitals plead for oxygen as more patients,' -BBC news.
    - → Karnataka- 24 people in ICU died.
    - → Delhi- 7 people died including a doctor.
- India facing vaccine shortage, oxygen shortage.
- Australia→ if anyone comes from India to Australia then 5 years of impression to them.
- Second wave of Corona is getting reduced.
- Tamil Nadu-20k cases reported in the last 24 hrs.

    -153 deaths in the past 24 hrs.

5th May

- 3 lakh affected cases, 3 thousand deaths in India.
- Affected cases in Karnataka→ 50 thousand, just in Bangalore→ 25 thousand cases.
- The government of India announced there is a high chance of a 3rd wave of Corona in future.
- Dr. K Vijay Raghavan announced, 'we need to be prepared for the third wave and the current vaccine needs to be upgraded to fight agents in the future Corona variants'.

8th May

- 4 lakh cases, 4,187 death in India,
    - → More than 15% positivity rate in 24 hrs.
    - → 35% positive rate in West Bengal.
    - → 35% positive rate in Delhi.
    - → 25% positive rate in Maharashtra.
    - → 25% positive rate in Karnataka.
    - → 15-20% Bihar, Uttar Pradesh.

12th May

- 3.48 lakh people were affected and 4,305 people died in India.
  * Karnataka 5 lakh.
  * Maharashtra 5 lakh.
  * Kerala 4 lakh.
  * Uttar Pradesh 2 lakh.
- 22% positive report in India.
- 'India variant hit 44 countries B1.617' by WHO.
- Dr. Fauci said 'India opened the lockdown thinking the first wave was over and if they had extended the second wave would have prevented'.
- IInd wave→ 45 days Shahid Jameel due to lack of seriousness.
- Maharashtra is going to extend the lockdown.

- WHO independent.
- 'Delay hesitation denial' was the reason Corona says China.

13th May

- 3,62 lakh cases, 4,110 deaths in India.
- The black fungus which is seen in trees started to affect humans, especially to those who are affected by Corona.
- The Union government stated 'within the end of this year 700 crore vaccines will be made in India.'
- The Corona cases internationally and in India are almost the same, the rates are the same.
- India the highest Corona-affected country.

26th May

- → 2.69 crore were affected, and 3 lakh died in India→ as per Indian media.
- → 70 crore were affected, and 42 lakh died in India→ as per New York Times.

27th May

- Dr. Fauci was asked in United Facts 'Do you really believe that lab theory is still a conspiracy theorist theory?' and he said 'no' {this was in 2020}.
- In November 2019, 3 people showed the symptoms of Covid-19 and were admitted to a nearby hospital (people from a virology lab). A total of 6 got admitted and recovered⇒ This news came in the Wall Street Journal last week.
- In 2012, few copper mine workers in China got affected by Corona while cleaning the copper mine and people from the Wuhan virology lab went and took many bats for research.
- Biden→ we are going to reach a lab theory in 90 days from our experts.
- WHO sent a term to China to find how Corona was started; most of the team didn't have proper freedom to do the research. The Chinese government was having control over them, and those papers suggested that the virus didn't get out of the lab. But the WHO head said, the Chinese government handed all the details so there must be a chance of getting things altered.
- Facebook used to remove the 'Corona from China lab' posts claiming its fake news, but now they changed.

- Tamil Nadu has the highest cases in India.

1st June

- A 41-year-old guy got admitted in Jiangsu province in China and was found to be affected by H10N3 for the first time ever. This bird flu was found in just 5-6 people in the past 40 years.
- Hospitals didn't allow the person to discharge, even though he was all set, the doctors kept for future observation. And they officially said 'No need to worry, it won't get to humans, just one got affected and we informed it that's it!'
- H10N3 was not found to be attacked in chickens.
- British professor 'Dr Birger Sorensen': 'Everything on earth has an ancestor and this Corona has no credible ancestor. And this has been made in China's lab and I can prove it scientifically.'
    - → There are researchers who mentioned this to the authorities and they have gone missing and this made a strong backbone to the lab theory.
    - → The speed of spread, mutation and the method of the nature of the virus made me research this and me to reach this conclusion: "They have altered the original virus."
- The U.S president gave 90 days time to put the report regarding the lab theory.

- All state governments had a talk of getting prepared for the 3rd wave so that they can control the situation and not to happen as it happened in the 1st wave.
- "The 3rd wave may be affecting children", says the experts.
- In Ahmednagar, Maharashtra 8 thousand kids have been Covid positive in the period of May1- May31.
- 1,27,510 cases have been submitted from the past 24 hrs in the whole of India.
- Tamil Nadu has the highest Covid cases, in just the last day 27,936 cases.

4th June

- The Union government suggested if a district has less than a 5% positivity rate from the past 7 days, then the place can unlock the lockdown.
- India's positive rate on 3rd June was 6.1%, Delhi and Mumbai Corona dropped.
- Just yesterday's affected rate in Delhi- 487.
- Fauci said in a press conference "3 people who got sick in Wuhan lab in 2019, their health reports need to be examined, and will decide about the lab theory."
- Donald Trump- "China should need to pay 10 trillion US dollars to the USA as compensation for spreading Corona."[6]
- 1.32 lakh affected cases in India.
  *22,651 cases in Tamil Nadu (highest affected in India).

---

[6] *Explained properly in 'Anoroc- Duo'*

10th June

- Death rates from the past 2-3 days are around 2,000 worldwide.
- The death rate today in India is 6,148.
- ·The High Court made a term to check the real death rates of Bihar and found a 72% increase and nationally it went from 2 thousand to 6 thousand.
  - → The death rates were around 5 thousand in Bihar and after the term found out it increased to 9 thousand. The rest of the 4 thousand has been mixed with the recovery rate to hide the real death rate. These 4 thousand people died in private hospitals and in houses.
- 94,052 cases have been reported today in India.
  *17,321 in Tamil Nadu.
  *16,204 in Kerala.
- Till 9th June 3.3% of people took the 2nd doses of vaccine and 14% took the 1st shot.

11th June

- Total of 91 thousand affected cases in India.

19th June

- As per the report at the end of July the third wave will start (in next 6-8 weeks).
- 60,753 reported cases, 1,647 deaths in India.
- In Telangana, there is no more lockdown from tomorrow, school, college are compulsory from July 1st.

23rd June

- 50 thousand reported in India.
- Delta plus has been announced as a 'variant of concern' by the WHO.
- 40 cases of Delta plus have been reported in India so far,
  * 2 Maharashtra.
  *6 Madhya Pradesh.
  *3 Kerala.
  *3 Tamil Nadu.
  *2 Karnataka.
  *1 Jammu Kashmir.
  *1 Punjab.
  *1 Andhra Pradesh.
- IITK term→ 3rd wave will be spotted in September or October. 2-5 lakh will be the peak affected rates (if the vaccine didn't work on the Delta plus variant).
- Lots of kids got admitted to hospitals in West Bengal.

25th June

- Africa is facing a lack of vaccinations.
- The date has been changed for the second dose of the vaccine to 85 days.
- 51,667 affected cases, and 1,329 death rates in India.
- 30%-40% of people vaccinated in an area can prevent Corona, but due to Delta plus 85%-90% should need to get vaccinated.

28th June

- 46,148 affected cases, 979 death cases in India.
  *Maharashtra- 9,974 cases.
- Delta Plus in 13 states; nationally 49 cases and 45 thousand samples.
- Dr. Vejenthra Singh→ as per ICMR internal data→ 70% of people are having immunity in India agents Corona.
- The 1st Delta plus case was reported in Rajasthan→ 65 year old females and she was already Corona affected earlier and had taken the two vaccines also, she didn't die.
- The vaccine is reducing the strength of the Delta plus variant.

1st July

- British→ Vaccine boosters need to be taken for more prevention agents Corona.
- Dr Fauci says there are going to be 2 Americas,
  1st= vaccinated.
  2nd= non-vaccinated (Vaccine hesitant).
- Cytomegalovirus (CMV)→ Ganga Ram hospital in Delhi, when Covid weakens the immunity of the person that CMV attacks.

10th July

- Death rates in India- 1,206, 13,563 reported cases in Kerala, 9k in Maharashtra, 3k in Tamil Nadu.
- Zika virus cases in Kerala jumped to 40.
- ❖ 1947→ Zika has been identified in monkeys in Zika forests, Uganda.

30th July

- Nanjing, China is under a strict lockdown just like the previous year's Wuhan scenario, but this time due to a new variant of Corona; The delta variant.
    - → As a precaution measure, everyone will be Corona tested in that area and even the people who visit in emergencies are also tested. And also tracking all the people left from that area to test them and to keep them under quarantine.

3rd August

- The Delta variant spreads faster than all the previous variants.
- China vaccinated more than 60% of the population. The Delta variant affected vaccinated people as well.
- Mid-summer was when Delta came, and as it was summer and a tourist area the people got affected more at that time, and that is how the government pointed out the spread of the Delta variant.
- If one person in an area gets affected by Corona then the whole area will be sealed as a precaution step. Due to this, the Chinese government announced that 'any person who recently goes out of their place should report for the check-up'.
- Corona spread from the airport in China.
- One woman who didn't show up in the Anti epidemic and disease prevention law.
- Kerala has the highest Corona rate in whole India.

6th August

- The Lamda variant was first formed in Peru, South America and full South America got affected and now the death rates are higher in South America.
- Vaccination won't work in the Lamda variant.
- Australia, Sidney in lockdown from past 6 weeks, still no decrease in cases, the variant cased in Delta, which has originated from India.
- Half of China is under lockdown due to the Deltha variant.
- The Lamda variant may cause the 3rd wave and cause big problems. Lamda has been put in a 'variant of interest'.
- 44,643 confirmed cases in India (Delta variant).
- Kerala→ 22 thousand (Delta variant).
- Top virologist cautions over 3rd wave in India to be Delta variant.
- 44,643- cases reported in India and in that, 22 thousand cases in Kerala. Maintaining 40 thousand from the past 2 months.
- In West Bengal, Mamtha Banerjee announced schools and colleges will be back to active after Durga pooja (after October 11-15).

13th August

- The Lamda variant affected 95% in South America.
- Peru has the highest death rate and the majority by the Lamda variant.
- The speciality of the Lamda variant is that it can neutralise the vaccine, which was found out by scientists from Japan.
- Delta plus was first identified in London, with 5 people. Those 5 people arrived from the Nepal area.
- The test sample that was sent on 23rd July was received on 13 August.
- 3 people from Mumbai died due to the Delta plus variant, the first death from this variant in India. One among those was a female who was fully vaccinated; she had phenomena and diabetics.
- 85 people got affected by the Delta plus variant.
  - *23 from Maharashtra.
  - *11 people from Madhya Pradesh.
  - *10 cases in Tamil Nadu.
  - *Rest 41 from other parts of India.
- No Lamda cases in India so far.

25th August

- A German scientist says that the chances for Covid-22 in future. 'Delta' variant from India, 'Beta' variant from South Africa, 'Gamma' variant from Peru, when all these get combined Covid-22 will be formed, and it will be a diabolic variant. And this gets passed by the people who all didn't take the vaccine.

❖ **So as per that scientist, the only way to save from this Covid-22 is to get vaccinated.**

- MHA (Ministry of Home Affairs) warns for the chances of the third wave of Covid-19 in September-October by:-
    → Scenario-1 if the current Delta variant gets mutated then the death rate will get high in future (3.2 lakh affected cases in October).
    → Scenario-2 if a new variant gets mutated and spreads in September then in one day the affected rate will be 5 lakh cases.
    → Scenario-3 October end third wave may happen and it's not strong, If it hits 2 lakh cases itself is a big deal. That will be a weak variant.
- WHO→ stop predicting the third waves and focus on getting vaccinated.

- WHO scientist Soumya Saminathan→ Corona issues have changed from epidemic to endemic in India. But taking the vaccination is the best way to protect from Corona attack.

3rd September

- 'Mu' variant has been found in Central America since January. And this will get affected by both people who took the vaccine and those who don't.
- Due to the 'Mu' variant, India made a 24 hr quarantine.
- India's third wave. With India recording over 47,000 Coronavirus cases in the last 24 hours, (the highest in two months). Scientists from Indian Council of Medical Research (ICMR) have suggested that states witnessing a hike in cases, should analyse local data to prepare for the third wave and limit virus spread.
- Southern states such as Kerala, Tamil Nadu and Karnataka have been recording the highest number of fresh Covid-19 infected cases in the past few weeks. "We will have to keep in mind while talking about the third wave of the Covid-19 pandemic in India, since the beginning of the pandemic, states have seen a heterogenous rise in cases.
- The off-line exam that was conducted by the state government for the eleventh standard students has been postponed by the Supreme court.
- More than 30 thousand cases per day in Kerala from the past 4 days.

- In India, 68% of the population has the antibody agent Corona.
  * Madhya Pradesh- 79%.
  * Tamil Nadu- 69%.
  * Kerala- 44%. And due to this is why Kerala has the highest Corona affected rate in India by ICMR.

25th September

- Australia still claims Corona as a man-made virus.
- Dr. Li Wenliang, a doctor in Wuhan hospital; in December 2019 he observed a rare condition in which 8 people got admitted to the hospital with a strange disease and after their blood test he concluded that there is a new virus roaming among people. And when he informed the authorities he was taken to the police station and warned him not to tell anyone about this and 'If you say anything about this virus, that doesn't exist then we will put you in jail' but the doctor pleaded that he is not lying and the virus really exists. Then the doctor got strict action that he can't go to work and can't talk to anyone.
- He died due to Corona after treating the Covid patients. And when the people in China found out about this the people made a big hubbub on their social media, claiming why did the government hide from the public.
- The other scientist and the doctor who went to America from China due to their treatment of life revealed that Coronavirus does exist in bats but if you research this you will understand that this virus had a

human touch, a man-altered virus and that's why it got spread worldwide.

- A document got leaked, that the Wuhan virology lab submitted a document, asking for funding for their research on Coronavirus that's been in the bats and to see what that newly modified virus can do, many opposed the funding, and one of the major companies that funded for this was the U.S. This happened 18 months before the Corona outbreak.

14th October

- 'Globally the countries that took the vaccination properly have the least chances to get hit by the third wave' -WHO.
- Cases higher in European countries, due to the lack of vaccination in Europe. Reason$\Rightarrow$ vaccination hesitation.
- And as per the experts even if the third wave happens the power of the vaccine will be lower.
- Chances to get 3rd wave in India, but more than 70% of the population took the first shot of the vaccine, and 29% took the second shot.
- The total count of vaccines taken in India is 96 crore.
- 'India reports 18,987 new Covid cases in the last 24 hrs, 20% higher than day before' - India today.

22th October

- In Russia and China half of the places are under lockdown.
- 1 thousand people are dying in Russia per day due to AY.4.2. And in the next 10 days they are going under lock down.
  - 36% of people took the 1st dose vaccine and the rest showed vaccination hesitancy and the public are not much wearing masks as well.
- Russia had opened tourism even before the second wave was over and that was the reason for the current Corona hike.
- Flights were cancelled and the school closed as China fights Covid-19 outbreak.
  - Beijing has a zero Corona policy.
- Moscow is closing schools, colleges and many businesses due to this virus.

25th October

- China locks down, expects new Covid out breaks to worsen in upcoming days.
- Russia records Coronavirus highest since the start of Covid-19 pandemic. (AY 4.2).
- More than 35% vaccinated in Russia, the people are not wearing masks and due to that one week of lockdown in total Russia.
  - The people can go to public places but need to show the vaccine passport.
- China is 75% vaccinated but still under strict lockdown.
- No major threads in India yet, Andrea Pradesh, Kerala, Jammu and Kashmir, Telegana, Maharashtra, Karnataka are currently showing the Corona cases, but under control.
- AY4.2, AY.33, AY 4.1 are recovering in India.
  - 17 people showed symptoms of AY4.2.
- In India the waves were: Corona→ Delta→ AY 4.2→ AY 4.1, AY.33.

1st November

- Shanghai Disneyland closed entirely because they found one single Covid-19 case. Total of 34 thousand people went under the Covid test. There was no positive case in the test but in pure doubt, the government made all the people stay in the house for the next 2 days.
- Three cities are under lockdown after 1 reported case.
- China vaccinated the most around 75% of the population.
- Corona vac and Sinopharm$\Rightarrow$ vaccines by China.
- China even made the traffic lights red to stop people from commuting.

14th November

- 'No classes and offices in Delhi from next week, government workers have to work from home' → due to air pollution.
- 40% of the air pollution is due to transportation.
- Industries depositing waste on Yamuna.

2 1th November

- Cases are high in European countries.
- In the Netherlands people threw stones at ambulances for vaccination hesitancy.
- Record highest cases in Europe, the government decided to start a small lockdown.
    - Austria officially announced by February 2022 all should be vaccinated→ and that's how the protest started.
- Disney halted the vaccine mandate for theme park workers after the Florida ban.
- In the last 60 days Corona cases in India have been dropping constantly.

26th November

- Covid: New heavily mutated variant B.1.1.529 in South Africa, raises concern.
    - The name of the virus is 'Nu'.
    - It's a variant of concern.
    - Israel detected the first case.
    - South Africa, Belgium, Israel, Botswana, Hong Kong started showing increased cases.

29th November

- A doctor from South America found a difference in Delta variant Corona in her patient on November 18 and that's when the Omicron variant was found. (Extreme tiredness was the symptom).
- As per the experts, the Delta variant has gone under 8 mutations whereas the Omicron has gone under 30.
- None died or any serious illness due to Omicron; just spreading like a forest fire.
- 'Nu' sounded like 'New' in English and 'Xi' is the name of the Chinese President; that is the reason why they skipped them in Greek alphabets and went to 'Omicron'.

1st December

- Soudi Arabia, Nigeria, UK, Japan, France, Israel, Czech Republic, Brazil, Netherland, Germany, HongKong, Canada, Australia, Portugal, Bostuvana, Spain, Belgium, Italy, Switzerland, and Austria are affected by the Omicron variant.
- There are no Omicron cases in China, India, U.S.
- Most Omicron cases are 'mild' and there's no evidence to suggest vaccines may be less effective against the variant' WHO officials.
- Bostuvana→ 3 people showed symptoms of Omicron, fever, throat pain→ normal common cold symptoms; the rest of the 2 people were asymptomatic.

2nd December

- India's first 2 Omicron cases in Bangalore, Karnataka; one is a foreigner.' -NDTV.
    - → One is a doctor who has symptoms and checks himself and goes under quarantine (40 years old).
    - → One is a foreigner who came from Africa and left India even before the result came out. He went to Dubai and from there he went to South Africa. (He was asymptomatic).

7th December

- No deaths due to Omicron globally so far.
- IMA gives a massive 3rd wave warning.
- Covid-19 third wave likely to hit India by February: IIT scientists warn of Omicron fears.

16th December

- 'Wuhan lab leak is the most likely to be the origin of Covid-19' -The telegraph.
- 'Covid-19 Omicron variants spread 70 times faster than Delta, study finds' -The Times of India.
- Tamil Nadu reported the first Omicron case in India.

22nd December

- The affected case is higher and death rates are lower in Africa.
- 'Omicron third wave in India, just a matter of time now' -The Economic times.

24th December

- Africa is less vaccinated but the deaths in Omicron are really less; on the other hand UK & US are highly vaccinated countries with highest death rates reported.
- Below 7 thousand affected cases in India.
- 'Over 350 Omicron cases in India are recovered, says the government' -The Times of India.
- Two weeks back it was 2 and now it's 350.
    - → In that 100 cases from Maharashtra.
    - → 34 from Tamil Nadu.
- Night curfews imposed in Hariyans, unvaccinated people are going to be banned from public places.
- Madhya Pradesh, Uttar Pradesh (from today) are having lockdowns.
- Maharashtra overnight gatherings are restricted and 50% restrictions to gyms, beauty parlours and theatres.
- Omicron may trigger a third wave in India, could be around Feb 3rd: IIT-K studies suggest this precaution.

129

THE END

Epilogue

2020

January

- January 1 – Croatia begins its term in the presidency of the European Union.
- January 2 - The Royal Australian Air Force and Navy are deployed to New South Wales to assist mass evacuation efforts amidst the 2019–20 Australian bushfire season.
- January 3 – 2019–2021 Persian Gulf crisis: A United States drone strike at Baghdad International Airport kills Iranian general Qasem Soleimani and Iraqi paramilitary leader Abu Mahdi al-Muhandis.
- January 5 – Second Libyan Civil War: President Recep Tayyip Erdoğan announces the deployment of Turkish troops to Libya on behalf of the United Nations-backed Government of National Accord.
- January 8
  - 2019–21 Persian Gulf crisis: Iran launches ballistic missiles at two Iraqi military bases hosting U.S. soldiers, injuring multiple personnel.
  - 2019–21 Persian Gulf crisis: Ukraine International Airlines Flight 752 is shot down by Iranian forces shortly after takeoff from Tehran Imam Khomeini International

Airport, killing all 176 people on board.

- January 9
  - A rare, circumbinary planet called TOI 1338-b is discovered.
  - Islamic State in the Greater Sahara militants assault a Nigerien military base in Chinagodrar, killing at least 89 Nigerien soldiers.
- January 10 – Haitham bin Tarik succeeds Qaboos bin Said as the Sultan of Oman.
- January 12 – The Taal Volcano in the Philippines has its first major eruption since 1977.
- January 16 – The first impeachment trial of the President of the United States, Donald Trump, begins in the U.S. Senate. He is acquitted on February 5.
- January 18 – Yemeni Civil War: 111 Yemeni soldiers and 5 civilians are killed in a drone and missile attack on a military camp near Ma'rib.
- January 20 – COVID-19 pandemic: Chinese authorities publicly confirm human-to-human transmission of severe acute respiratory syndrome coronavirus 2.
- January 23 – COVID-19 pandemic: The Chinese city of Wuhan, the epicentre of the initial COVID-19 outbreak, is

quarantined with all scheduled public transport services and intercity flights halted.

- January 29 – U.S. president Donald Trump signs the United States–Mexico–Canada Agreement, a North American trade agreement set to replace NAFTA.
- January 30 – COVID-19 pandemic: The World Health Organization (WHO) declares the outbreak of the disease as a Public Health Emergency of International Concern, the sixth time that this measure has been invoked since 2009.
- January 31 – The United Kingdom and Gibraltar formally withdraw from the European Union, beginning an 11-month transition period.

February

- February 11 – COVID-19 pandemic: The World Health Organization (WHO) names the disease COVID-19.
- February 13 – NASA publishes a detailed study of Arrokoth, the most distant body ever explored by a spacecraft.
- February 24 – The Pakatan Harapan coalition government of Malaysia collapses and is replaced by the Perikatan Nasional coalition. Muhyiddin Yassin becomes the eighth Prime Minister of Malaysia on 1 March.
- February 27 – 2020 stock market crash: Triggered by fears of the spreading of COVID-19, the Dow Jones Industrial Average (DJIA) plunges by 1,190.95 points, or 4.4%, to close at 25,766.64, its largest one-day point decline at the time. This follows several days of large falls, marking the worst week for the index since 2008.
- February 28 – Syrian Civil War: NATO expresses solidarity with Turkey after 34 Turkish soldiers were killed in an airstrike by pro-Syrian government forces.
- February 29 – A conditional peace agreement is signed between the United States and the Taliban. The U.S. begins

gradually withdrawing combat troops from Afghanistan on March 10.

March

- March 5 – The International Criminal Court authorizes the Afghanistan War Crimes inquiry to proceed, reportedly allowing for the first time for U.S. citizens to be investigated.
- March 9
    - COVID-19 pandemic: Italy becomes the first country to implement a nationwide quarantine in response to the COVID-19 outbreak.
    - International share prices fall sharply in response to a Russo-Saudi oil price war and the impact of COVID-19. The Dow Jones Industrial Average (DJIA) plunges more than 2,000 points, the largest fall in its history up to that point. Oil prices also plunge by as much as 30% in early trading, the biggest fall since 1991.
- March 11 – COVID-19 pandemic: The World Health Organization declares the COVID-19 outbreak a pandemic.
- March 12 – Global stock markets crash due to the COVID-19 pandemic and the United States travel ban on the Schengen Area. The DJIA goes into free fall, closing at over −2,300 points, the worst losses for the index since 1987.

- March 13 – COVID-19 pandemic: The government of Nepal announces that Mount Everest will be closed to climbers and the public for the rest of the season due to concerns from the COVID-19 pandemic in Asia.
- March 16 – The Dow Jones Industrial Average falls by 2,997.10, the single largest point drop in history and the second-largest percentage drop ever at 12.93%, an even greater crash than Black Monday (1929). This follows the U.S. Federal Reserve announcing that it will cut its target interest rate to 0–0.25%.
- March 17
  - COVID-19 pandemic:
  - The European Union's external and Schengen borders are closed for at least 30 days in an effort to curb the COVID-19 pandemic.
  - The Euro 2020 and 2020 Copa América association football tournaments are postponed until the summer of 2021 by UEFA and CONMEBOL respectively.
- March 18
  - COVID-19 pandemic:
  - The Eurovision Song Contest 2020 is cancelled due to COVID-19 in Europe, the first cancellation in the contest's 64-year history.

- o Solidarity trial, a WHO-sponsored clinical trial dedicated to finding a cure against COVID-19, is announced.
- March 20
  - o COVID-19 pandemic: The worldwide death toll from COVID-19 surpasses 10,000 as the total number of cases reaches a quarter of a million.
  - o The Bhadla Solar Park is commissioned and becomes the world's largest solar park.
- March 24
  - o COVID-19 pandemic:
  - o India and the United Kingdom go into lockdown to contain COVID-19. The total number of people in the world facing some form of pandemic-related movement restriction now exceeds 2.6 billion, a third of the global population.
  - o Chinese Premier Li Keqiang reports that the domestically transmitted epidemic is now under control. Two days later, China temporarily suspends entry for foreign nationals with visas or residence permits, effective midnight March 28.
  - o The International Olympic Committee and Japan suspend the 2020 Summer Olympics until 2021. On March 30, the Summer Olympics

are rescheduled from July 23 to August 8, 2021.

- March 26
  - COVID-19 pandemic:
  - Global COVID-19 cases reach 500,000, with nearly 23,000 deaths confirmed. The U.S. surpasses China and Italy in total number of known COVID-19 cases, with at least 81,321 cases and more than 1,000 deaths.
  - Militants in the Philippines, Syria, Yemen, and Libya agree to U.N. Secretary-General António Guterres' call for a ceasefire; some accept medical aid for themselves and civilians in their communities. Colombia and Venezuela discuss a common response to the global pandemic, and the UAE airlifts aid to Iran.
- March 27 – North Macedonia becomes the 30th country to join NATO.
- March 30 – 2020 Russia–Saudi Arabia oil price war: The price of Brent Crude falls 9% to $23 per barrel, the lowest level since November 2002.

April

- April 1
  - COVID-19 pandemic: China reports 130 asymptomatic cases of COVID-19, its first reported asymptomatic cases.
    - Yemen's internationally recognised government releases more than 470 of its prisoners amid concerns of the spread of the virus in Yemen's overcrowded jails. The United Nations Human Rights Council has called for the release of all political prisoners.
- April 2 – COVID-19 pandemic: The number of confirmed cases of COVID-19 passes 1 million worldwide.
- April 5
  - COVID-19 pandemic:
    - The first case of COVID-19 in a zoo animal is reported: a four-

year-old female Malayan tiger at the Bronx Zoo in New York City.

- April 6 – The United States designates the Russian Imperial Movement as a terrorist organization and imposes sanctions on its leaders; it is the first white supremacist group the U.S. has designated as a terrorist organization.
- April 7 – COVID-19 pandemic: Japan declares a state of emergency in response to COVID-19 and finalises a stimulus package worth 108 trillion yen (US$990 billion), equal to 20% of the country's GDP.
- April 8 - COVID-19 pandemic: The Saudi-led coalition declares a unilateral ceasefire in its operations against Houthi forces in Yemen in accordance with United Nations-led efforts.
- April 10
    - Kivu Ebola epidemic: The Democratic Republic of the Congo reports the first case of Ebola since February 2020. The outbreak has killed more than 2,200 people since August 2018.
    - The ESA/JAXA space probe BepiColombo makes its final gravity assist around Earth and begins to depart for

Venus, where it will make several gravity assist maneuvers before finally arriving at Mercury in 2025.

- COVID-19 pandemic:
  - The death toll from COVID-19 exceeds 100,000 globally, a ten-fold increase from March 20.
  - EU finance ministers agree on a €540 billion loan package to alleviate the economic fallout of the coronavirus pandemic.

- April 12
  - COVID-19 pandemic: Pope Francis live streams the *Urbi et Orbi* blessing for Easter; it is the second blessing in a month, with the first taking place on March 27 during a special prayer service for the end of the pandemic.
  - OPEC and allies strike a deal to cut oil production by 9.7 million barrels per day, the largest such cut agreed upon, starting May 1.

- April 14
  - COVID-19 pandemic
    - The International Monetary Fund (IMF) says it expects the world economy to shrink 3%, the worst contraction since the Great Depression of the 1930s.
    - U.S. president Donald Trump announces that the U.S. will suspend funding towards the World Health Organization (WHO) pending an investigation of its handling of the COVID-19 pandemic and its relationship with China.
- April 15
  - COVID-19 pandemic:
    - The number of confirmed cases of COVID-19 passes 2 million worldwide.

- ▪ The 2020 Tour de France is delayed until August 2020 due to the COVID-19 pandemic.

- April 17
  - o The China Securities Regulatory Commission approves a transaction in which Switzerland's Credit Suisse will take a majority interest in a China securities firm, making Credit Suisse the first foreign bank to own a majority of such a company since the easing of foreign ownership rules in 2018.
  - o COVID-19 pandemic:
  - o China revises the COVID-19 death toll in Wuhan upward, adding 1,290 more fatalities to bring the country's reported COVID-19 deaths to 4,632.
  - o Europe surpasses 100,000 COVID-19-related deaths.
  - o The U.N. Human Rights Office accuses Myanmar of carrying out daily airstrikes in the Rakhine and Chin states and that at least 32 civilians have been killed since March 23. The separatist Arakan Army unilaterally declared a month-long ceasefire to fight the pandemic,

but the military rejected the ceasefire claiming a previous ceasefire had been reneged by the insurgents.

- April 18 – 44 suspected Boko Haram members are found dead, apparently due to poisoning, inside a prison in N'Djamena, Chad.
- April 19
    - Vietnam condemns China's prior decision to establish administrative districts in the disputed Paracel and Spratly Islands as a violation of its sovereignty.
    - COVID-19 pandemic: Unrest breaks out in Paris, Berlin and Vladikavkaz as opposition to COVID-19 lockdowns continue.
- April 20
    - Oil prices reach a record low, with West Texas Intermediate falling into negative values.
    - The Industrial Bank of Korea agrees to pay US$86 million and will enter a two-year deferred prosecution agreement to settle lawsuits with the U.S. Department of Justice and the state of New York over a 2011 scheme to help transfer US$1 billion to Iran.

- o Israeli Prime Minister Benjamin Netanyahu and Blue and White Alliance leader Benny Gantz agree on a deal to form a unity government, thus ending more than a year of political deadlock. As part of the deal, Netanyahu will hold onto his position for 18 more months, with Gantz replacing him afterwards.
- April 21 – Mozambique police say 52 male villagers were killed by Islamist militants earlier this month in Muidumbe District, Cabo Delgado Province, after they refused to join their ranks.
- April 22 – Iran's Islamic Revolutionary Guard Corps deploys the country's first military satellite, using a new satellite carrier called "Ghased" ("Messenger").
- April 23
  - o Syrian Civil War: Two former high-ranking members of the Syrian Army go on trial in Koblenz, Germany, for alleged war crimes committed during the civil war. It is the first time that Syrian military officials are prosecuted for their roles in the conflict.

- o COVID-19 pandemic: Facebook removes "pseudoscience" and "conspiracy theory" as options for targeted ads as criticism mounts against social media for its role in spreading misinformation about COVID-19.
- April 25
  - o Yemeni Civil War: The Southern Transitional Council (STC) announces the establishment of a self-rule administration in southern Yemen and deploys forces in Aden. Governors of multiple southern Yemeni Governorates and Socotra island reject the STC's claim to self-rule and declare their loyalty to President Abdrabbuh Mansur Hadi. Months later on July 19, the STC accepts a Saudi-brokered peace deal and abandons its self-rule aspirations.
  - o COVID-19 pandemic: The global death toll from COVID-19 exceeds 200,000. The UK becomes the fifth

country to report 20,000 deaths.

- April 26 – King Salman issues a royal decree, declaring that people will no longer be executed in Saudi Arabia for crimes they were convicted of when they were minors.
- April 27 – COVID-19 pandemic: The number of confirmed cases passes 3 million worldwide, while the number of confirmed cases in the U.S. passes 1 million.
- April 28
  - A fast radio burst is detected from the Magnetar SGR 1935+2154, the first ever detected inside the Milky Way, and the first to be linked to a known source.
  - Colombia formalizes its membership with the Organisation for Economic Co-operation and Development (OECD), becoming the 37th nation of the organization.
  - The Indian Ministry of External Affairs condemns the U.S. Commission on International Religious Freedom after its annual report recommends placing India on the "countries of

particular concern" blacklist over the Citizenship Amendment Act, the revocation of Jammu and Kashmir's special status, and controversial comments made by Home Minister Amit Shah, among others.

- April 29 – (52768) 1998 OR2, a near-Earth asteroid that is 2 kilometers (1.2 mi) wide, makes a close approach of 0.042 AU (6.3 million km; 16 LD) to Earth. It will not approach closer than this until 2079.
- April 30
    - NASA officially selects SpaceX, Blue Origin, and Dynetics to build its next-generation lunar lander to carry American astronauts to the Moon by 2024.
    - Bulgaria applies for ERM II (the "waiting room" for the Eurozone), due to join along with Croatia in July 2020.

May

- May 1 – COVID-19 pandemic: The total number of recovered COVID-19 patients reaches 1 million worldwide, according to data from The Johns Hopkins University.
- May 3–4 – Venezuelan dissidents and an American-based private military company, Silvercorp USA, unsuccessfully attempt to infiltrate Venezuela and forcibly remove President Nicolás Maduro from office.
- May 4 – A team of British and Kenyan scientists announce the discovery of Microsporidia MB, a parasitic microbe in the Microsporidia fungi group that blocks mosquitos from carrying malaria, potentially paving the way for the control of malaria.
- May 5
    - COVID-19 pandemic: The U.K. death toll from COVID-19 becomes the highest in Europe at 32,313 after exceeding the death toll of 29,029 in Italy.
    - The Philippines' National Telecommunications Commission issues a cease and desist order to the broadcasting operations of ABS-CBN, the country's largest media network, as

Congress fails to renew its franchise granted on March 30, 1995. The last time the network was shut down was upon the declaration of martial law by President Ferdinand Marcos in 1972. On July 10, members of the Philippine House Committee on Legislative Franchises vote against the franchise renewal of the said network.

- May 6
    - Astronomers announce the discovery of the first black hole located in a star system visible to the naked eye.
    - COVID-19 pandemic: New evidence indicates that an Algerian-born French fishmonger, who had not traveled to China and did not have contact with any Chinese nationals, was treated for pneumonia from an unknown source on December 27, 2019, now identified as COVID-19.
- May 9 – Several Chinese and Indian soldiers are injured in a cross-border clash at the Nathu La crossing. About 150 troops participated in the face-off,

which involved fistfights and stone-throwing.

- May 10
  - The Iranian Navy frigate *Jamaran* accidentally strikes the Iranian support vessel *Konarak* with a missile, killing nineteen sailors. This is the first friendly fire incident since February 2019, when an Indian Mil Mi-17 helicopter was mistakenly shot down by Indian air defense forces.
  - COVID-19 pandemic: Wuhan reports its first coronavirus cases in more than a month. An 89-year-old man is confirmed positive, but his wife and several members of the community are recorded as asymptomatic cases.
- May 11 – The Max Planck Institute for Evolutionary Anthropology publishes the result of radiocarbon and DNA analysis from the fossils that has been found in the Bacho Kiro cave, Bulgaria. The result, showing that the fossils belong to *Homo sapiens* instead of Neanderthal, indicates that modern humans may have arrived in Europe thousands of years earlier than previously thought.

- May 12 – Gunmen storm a maternity hospital and kill 24 people, including two newborn babies, in Dashte Barchi, a majority-Shia neighborhood of Kabul, Afghanistan. In a separate incident in Kuz Kunar, 32 people are killed at a funeral by a suicide bomber.
- May 14
    - COVID-19 pandemic:
        - The global death toll from COVID-19 exceeds 300,000.
        - The UN warns of a global mental health crisis caused by isolation, fear, uncertainty and economic turmoil.
    - NATO Secretary General Jens Stoltenberg says the military alliance is "ready to support" the UN-recognized Government of National Accord while Greece, a member state of NATO, strongly criticizes Stoltenberg's remarks, saying his recognition of the "Muslim Brotherhood government" does not reflect

        the positions of the military alliance.

- May 15 – Researchers announce a 2.5 cm millipede fossil belonging to the *Kampecaris* genus, discovered on the island of Kerrera in the Scottish Inner Hebrides, is the world's oldest-known land animal, which lived 425 million years ago in the Silurian period.
- May 16
    - COVID-19 pandemic: Bundesliga becomes the first major sports league to resume its season since March 11.
    - Félicien Kabuga, a Rwandan businessman responsible for supporting the Rwandan genocide, is arrested in Asnières-sur-Seine, France, after 26 years as a fugitive.
- May 18
    - The United Nations Office for the Coordination of Humanitarian Affairs announces that nearly 1 million people are affected and at least 24 people have died in flash floods that have hit Beledweyne and Jowhar, Somalia.
    - In a historic move, the World Health Organization holds its annual World Health

Assembly using video conferencing instead of in-person meetings.

- May 19 – Palestinian President Mahmoud Abbas announces the termination of all agreements, including security ones, with Israel and the United States in response to Israel's plans to annex the Jordan Valley.
- May 21
    - Cyclone Amphan makes landfall in eastern India and Bangladesh, killing over 100 people and forcing the evacuation of more than 4 million others. It causes over US$13 billion in damage, making it the costliest cyclone ever recorded in the North Indian Ocean, shattering the record previously held by Nargis.
    - The U.S. announces it will withdraw from the Open Skies Treaty within six months, alleging continuous violations by Russia.
    - COVID-19 pandemic: The number of confirmed cases of COVID-19 passes 5 million worldwide, with 106,000 new cases recorded over the past

24 hours, the highest single-day figure so far.

- May 22
  - Flight PK8303, a Pakistan International Airlines passenger aircraft, crashes in a residential area near Karachi, in Pakistan, killing 97 of the 99 total people on board and injuring dozens on the ground.
  - COVID-19 pandemic: Brazil overtakes Russia to become the country with the second highest number of COVID-19 cases, with over 330,000 reported. President Jair Bolsonaro continues to dismiss the threat of the virus.
- May 23 – COVID-19 pandemic: China reports no new cases for the first time since the pandemic began, according to the National Health Commission.
- May 24
  - Mining corporation Rio Tinto admits to blowing up the 46,000-year-old Juukan Gorge caves in the Pilbara area of Western Australia. The firm later issues an apology to the two Aboriginal peoples who are the traditional owners of the site.

- o Egyptian President Abdel Fattah el-Sisi pardons 3,157 prisoners to celebrate Eid al-Fitr and, two days later, President of Zambia Edgar Lungu pardons nearly 3,000 inmates to commemorate Africa Freedom Day.
- May 26
  - o Protests caused by the murder of George Floyd break out across hundreds of cities in the U.S. and around the world. These are followed by further protests and rallies on June 6 against racism and police brutality around the world.
  - o Costa Rica becomes the first Central American country to legalise same-sex marriage.
  - o LATAM Airlines, the largest air carrier in Latin America, files for Chapter 11 bankruptcy.
- May 27
  - o The Chinese National People's Congress votes in favour of national security legislation that criminalizes "secession", "subversion", "terrorism" and foreign interference in Hong Kong;

the legislation grants sweeping powers to the Chinese central government to suppress the Hong Kong democracy movement, including banning activist groups and curtailing civil liberties. The U.S. government responds by declaring Hong Kong is "no longer autonomous" under the United States-Hong Kong Policy Act.

- COVID-19 pandemic: The U.S. death toll passes 100,000 – more Americans than were killed in the Vietnam War and Korean War combined, and approaching that of the First World War, where 116,000 Americans died in combat. The total number of cases continues to rise, although the rate is slowing.

- May 30 – The first crewed flight of the SpaceX Dragon 2 is launched from Cape Canaveral, Florida, the first manned spacecraft to take off from U.S. soil since the retirement of the Space Shuttle in 2011.

June

- June 1 – Kivu Ebola epidemic: The World Health Organization reports six new cases of Ebola, and UNICEF reports five deaths, in a renewed outbreak of the disease in Mbandaka, Équateur Province, Democratic Republic of the Congo.
- June 2 – A US$5 billion class action lawsuit is filed against Alphabet Inc. and Google, alleging the company violates users' right to privacy by tracking them in Chrome's incognito mode.
- June 3
  - Prime Minister Boris Johnson says the UK will change immigration laws to offer a pathway to UK citizenship for all Hong Kong citizens who are eligible for BN(O) status if the government of China imposes new security laws on the territory.
  - SpaceX successfully launches and deploys 60 Starlink satellites into a low Earth orbit from Cape Canaveral Air Force Station, bringing the total number of Starlink satellites in orbit to 482.
  - Russian President Vladimir Putin declares a state of emergency after 20,000 tons

of oil leaked into the Ambarnaya River near the Siberian city of Norilsk within the Arctic Circle on May 26, 2020. The World Wildlife Fund said the accident is believed to be the second-largest in modern Russian history.

- June 4
  - Libya's Government of National Accord (GNA) says they are in full control of the capital, Tripoli, after forces of the Libyan National Army (LNA) retreat from the territory following months of intense fighting in the city.
  - Hong Kong legislative council passed the controversial National Anthem Ordinance.
- June 7 – COVID-19 pandemic: The global death toll from COVID-19 exceeds 400,000.
- June 8 – COVID-19 pandemic: The number of confirmed cases of COVID-19 passes 7 million worldwide.
- June 9 –
  - COVID-19 pandemic: A Harvard University study suggests that COVID-19 may have been spreading in China

as early as August 2019, based on hospital car park usage and web search trends.

- June 15
    - At least 20 Indian soldiers and over 40 Chinese forces are killed or injured in skirmishes in the disputed Galwan Valley, the largest escalation along the Sino-Indian border in five decades.
    - Turkish and Iranian forces commence air and artillery strikes against Kurdistan Workers' Party forces in Iraqi Kurdistan. Turkey launches a land operation in the region on June 17.
- June 16
    - COVID-19 pandemic: The number of confirmed cases of COVID-19 passes 8 million worldwide.
    - North Korea demolishes the Inter-Korean Liaison Office in Kaesong, established in 2018 to improve relations.
- June 21 –

    An annular solar eclipse occurs.
- June 22 –

    COVID-19 pandemic: The number of confirmed cases of

COVID-19 passes 9 million worldwide.
- June 23 –
  - A 7.5-magnitude earthquake strikes the coast of Oaxaca, Mexico and kills at least four people. It is felt more than 640 kilometres (400 mi) away in Mexico City.
- June 27 – Micheál Martin succeeds Leo Varadkar as Taoiseach of Ireland, with Varadkar becoming Tánaiste in a historic three-party coalition government.
- June 28
  - COVID-19 pandemic:
    - The number of confirmed cases of COVID-19 passes 10 million worldwide. The U.S. continues to report the highest number of any country as it reaches 2.5 million, a quarter of all cases globally.
    - The global death toll from COVID-19 exceeds 500,000.

- June 30 – China passes the controversial Hong Kong national security law, allowing China to crack down on opposition to Beijing at home or abroad.

July

- July 1 – Russian voters back a constitutional amendment that, among other things, enables Vladimir Putin to seek two further six-year terms when his current term ends in 2024, potentially allowing him to remain in power until 2036.
- July 7
  - Protests begin throughout Bulgaria with the goal of removing Borisov's cabinet and Chief Prosecutor Ivan Geshev from office.
  - COVID-19 pandemic: Thousands of people rally outside the House of the National Assembly of Serbia in Belgrade in response to stricter lockdown measures proposed by President Aleksandar Vučić following an increase of cases in the city.
- July 8 – At least 180 bodies are found in mass graves in Djibo, Burkina Faso, where soldiers are fighting jihadists. It is suspected that government forces were involved in mass extrajudicial executions.
- July 10
  - The ECB accepts Bulgaria and Croatia into ERM II, a

       mandatory stage for countries wishing to adopt the euro. This is the currency union's first major expansion in half a decade.

       o Turkey's President Recep Tayyip Erdoğan orders the Hagia Sophia in Istanbul to be reverted to a mosque following a supreme court annulment of a 1934 presidential decree that made it into a museum.

- July 12 – China reports 141 dead or missing in floods since June; 28,000 homes have been damaged.
- July 15 – The Twitter accounts of prominent political figures, CEOs, and celebrities are hacked to promote a bitcoin scam.
- July 19 – Flooding of the Brahmaputra River kills 189 and leaves 4 million homeless in India and Nepal.
- July 21 – COVID-19 pandemic: European leaders agree to create a €750 billion (US$858 billion) recovery fund to rebuild EU economies impacted by the pandemic.
- July 22 – COVID-19 pandemic: The number of confirmed cases of COVID-19 passes 15 million worldwide.
- July 25 – COVID-19 pandemic: North Korean leader Kim Jong-un convenes an

emergency meeting, declares a state of emergency, and orders the lockdown of Kaesong after a person suspected of having COVID-19 returned from South Korea. If confirmed, it would be the first case to be officially acknowledged by North Korea.

- 28 July – Former Prime Minister of Malaysia Najib Razak is found guilty of all seven charges in the first of five trials on the 1MDB scandal, being jailed 12 years and fined RM210 million as a result.
- July 30 – NASA successfully launches its Mars 2020 rover mission to search for signs of ancient life and collect samples for return to Earth. The mission includes technology demonstrations to prepare for future human missions.

August

- August 1 – The Barakah nuclear power plant in the UAE becomes operational following delays since 2017. It is the first commercial nuclear power station in the Arab world.
- August 2 – COVID-19 pandemic: In rare talks, Emirati Foreign Minister Sheikh Abdullah bin Zayed Al Nahyan and Iranian Foreign Minister Mohammad Javad Zarif hold a video call to discuss various regional issues, including combating COVID-19 in their respective countries.
- August 4 – An explosion caused by unsafely stored ammonium nitrate kills over 220 people, injures thousands, and severely damages the port in Beirut, Lebanon. Damage is estimated at $10–15 billion, and an estimated 300,000 people are left homeless. The following day, the Lebanese government declares a two-week state of emergency.
- August 5 – U.S. Secretary of Health and Human Services Alex Azar travels to Taiwan, the highest U.S. official visit to the country in 40 years. The PRC condemns the visit.
- August 7 – Air India Express Flight 1344 crashes after overrunning the runway at Calicut International Airport in Kerala, India, killing 19 of the 191 people on board.

- August 9 – A presidential election in Belarus which led to incumbent Alexander Lukashenko's reelection sparks protests throughout the country after major opposition candidate Sviatlana Tsikhanouskaya rejected the results. Seven days later, the largest political march in Belarusian history takes place, with an estimated 300,000 people in Minsk and 200,000 in other Belarusian cities and towns.
- August 10 – COVID-19 pandemic: The number of confirmed cases of COVID-19 passes 20 million worldwide.
- August 11 – COVID-19 pandemic: Russian President Vladimir Putin announces that Russia has approved the world's first COVID-19 vaccine.
- August 13 – Israel and the UAE agree to normalise relations, marking the third Israel–Arab peace deal.
- August 15 – The Japanese bulk carrier *Wakashio*, which stranded on a reef in Mauritius last month, breaks in half. Approximately 1,000 tonnes of oil are spilled into the ocean, becoming the largest environmental disaster in the history of Mauritius.
- August 18 – A mutiny in a military base by soldiers of the Malian Armed Forces develops into a coup d'état. President Ibrahim Boubacar Keïta and Prime Minister Boubou Cissé, among other

senior governmental and military officers, are arrested. The next day, Keïta announces his resignation on state television.

- August 19 – The Special Tribunal for Lebanon convicts *in absentia* Salim Ayyash, a senior member of Hezbollah, for the 2005 assassination of former Prime Minister Rafic Hariri.
- August 22 – COVID-19 pandemic: The worldwide death toll from COVID-19 exceeds 800,000.
- August 23 – Bayern Munich wins the 2019–20 UEFA Champions League by beating Paris Saint-Germain in the final.
- August 25 – Africa is declared free of wild polio, the second virus to be eradicated from the continent since smallpox 40 years previously.
- August 26 – Amazon CEO Jeff Bezos becomes the first person in history to have a net worth exceeding US$200 billion, according to *Forbes*.
- August 27 – Hurricane Laura makes landfall in Lake Charles, Louisiana with winds of 150 mph, making it the strongest hurricane to ever strike the state in terms of windspeed, tied with the 1856 Last Island Hurricane.
- August 28 – Japanese Prime Minister Shinzo Abe, the longest-serving prime minister in the history of Japan,

announces his resignation from office, citing ill health.

- August 30 – COVID-19 pandemic: The number of confirmed cases of COVID-19 passes 25 million worldwide. India continues to record the highest daily increase of cases.

September

- September 3
  - Sudanese Prime Minister Abdalla Hamdok and Abdelaziz al-Hilu, the leader of the Sudan People's Liberation Movement-North (SPLM–N), sign an agreement to transition the country into a secular state. The agreement comes three days after the signing of a peace deal between Sudan's transitional government and the Sudan Revolutionary Front, which the SPLM–N opted out of. Weeks later on October 3, the transitional government signed a peace deal with the main rebel groups, including the Sudan People's Liberation Movement-North, which had refused to engage in previous talks.
  - The skeletons of 200 mammoths and 30 other animals are unearthed at a construction site for the Mexico City Santa Lucía Airport. It is the largest find of mammoth bones to date, surpassing The Mammoth

> Site in the U.S. which had 61 skeletons.

- September 4
  - Pope Benedict XVI becomes the longest-lived pope at 93 years, four months, and 16 days, surpassing Pope Leo XIII, who died in 1903.
  - The La Línea highway tunnel, the longest road tunnel in South America at a length of 8.65 kilometres (5.37 mi), is opened in Colombia after 14 years of construction and several delays.
  - Kosovo and Serbia announce that they will normalize economic relations. The two countries will also move their Israeli embassies to Jerusalem, becoming the third and fourth countries to recognize Jerusalem as Israel's capital.
  - Bahrain and Israel agree to normalise relations, marking the fourth Israel–Arab peace deal.
- September 6 – Typhoon Haishen makes landfall on Japan and then South Korea as a strong category 2-equivalent typhoon. It later makes landfall on North

Korea where widespread flooding occurs.

- September 14
  - The Royal Astronomical Society announces the detection of phosphine in Venus' atmosphere, which is known to be a strong predictor for the presence of microbial life.
  - The first discovery of the perfectly preserved remains of a cave bear, believed to be 22,000 to 39,500 years old (Late Pleistocene), is made in Lyakhovsky Islands, Siberia in the thawing permafrost.
- September 16
  - A United Nations Human Rights Council fact-finding mission formally accuses the Venezuelan government of crimes against humanity, including cases of killings, torture, violence against political opposition and disappearances since 2014. President Nicolás Maduro and other senior Venezuelan officials are among those implicated in the charges.

- - Yoshihide Suga becomes the new Prime Minister of Japan, replacing Shinzo Abe.
  - Hurricane Sally makes landfall on the Alabama coast as a high-end Category 2 hurricane, causing over $8 billion in damages and killing 8 people.
- September 17
  - - France, Germany, and the United Kingdom issue a joint *note verbale* to the United Nations rejecting China's claims to the South China Sea, and supporting the ruling in *Philippines v. China* that said the historic rights per the nine-dash line ran counter to the United Nations Convention on the Law of the Sea. However the statement says that on "territorial sovereignty" they "take no position".
    - COVID-19 pandemic: The number of confirmed cases of COVID-19 passes 30 million worldwide.
- September 19 – A 1634 edition of *The Two Noble Kinsmen*, the last play by English playwright William Shakespeare, is discovered at the Royal

Scots College's library in Salamanca, Spain. It is believed to be the oldest copy of any of his works in the country.

- September 20 – *BuzzFeed News* and the International Consortium of Investigative Journalists (ICIJ) release the FinCEN Files, a collection of 2,657 documents relating to the Financial Crimes Enforcement Network describing over 200,000 suspicious transactions valued at over US$2 trillion that occurred from 1999 to 2017 across multiple global financial institutions.

- September 21 – Microsoft agrees to buy video game holding company ZeniMax Media, including Bethesda Softworks and their following subsidiaries for US$7.5 billion, in what is the biggest and most expensive takeover in the history of the video game industry.

- September 27 – Deadly clashes erupt in Nagorno-Karabakh between Armenian and Azerbaijani forces. Armenia, Azerbaijan, and the Republic of Artsakh introduce martial law and mobilize forces.

- September 29
  - COVID-19 pandemic: The worldwide death toll from COVID-19 exceeds one million.
  - The Emir of Kuwait Sheikh Sabah al-Sabah dies at the

age of 91. Crown Prince Nawaf Al-Ahmad Al-Jaber Al-Sabah is named his successor.

October

- October 1 – The EU began legal proceedings against the UK after it ignored their deadline to drop controversial sections from its internal market Bill.
- October 5 – COVID-19 pandemic: The number of confirmed cases of COVID-19 passes 35 million worldwide. The news coincides with the World Health Organization estimating that total worldwide cases may be around 760 million - roughly a tenth of the global population.
- October 10 – Armenia and Azerbaijan agree on a ceasefire in the ongoing Nagorno-Karabakh conflict.
- October 15:
  - 2020 Thai protests: The Government of Thailand declares a "severe" state of emergency banning gatherings of five or more people, initiating a crackdown on demonstrations and imposing media censorship.
  - President of Kyrgyzstan Sooronbay Jeenbekov resigns from office after weeks of massive protests in the wake of the October 2020 parliamentary election;

- opposition leader Sadyr Japarov assumes office as both the acting president and Prime Minister of Kyrgyzstan.
- October 17 – 2020 New Zealand general election: Jacinda Ardern's Labour Party wins a landslide second term in office, defeating the National Party led by Judith Collins and gaining the country's first parliamentary majority since the introduction of the MMP voting system.
- October 19 – COVID-19 pandemic: The number of confirmed cases of COVID-19 passes 40 million worldwide.
- October 20 – NASA's OSIRIS-REx spacecraft briefly touches down on Bennu, becoming the agency's first probe to retrieve samples from an asteroid, with its cargo due for return to Earth in 2023.
- October 22 – The Geneva Consensus Declaration on Promoting Women's Health and Strengthening the Family is signed by government representatives from 34 countries.
- October 23
  - At the end of an 11-year demining process, the Falkland Islands are declared free of land mines, 38 years after the end of the 1982 war.

- o Israel and Sudan agree to normalise relations, marking the fifth Israel–Arab peace deal.
- October 26 – NASA confirms the existence of molecular water on the sunlit side of the Moon, near Clavius crater, at concentrations of up to 412 parts per million.
- October 29 – The International Organization for Migration (IOM) confirms the death of least 140 migrants who drowned off the coast of Senegal on a vessel bound for the Spanish Canary Islands. It is the deadliest shipwreck of 2020 so far.
- October 30
  - o 2020 Aegean Sea earthquake: A magnitude 7.0 earthquake hits Turkey and Greece, killing 119 people and injuring over 1,000.
  - o COVID-19 pandemic: The number of confirmed cases of COVID-19 passes 45 million worldwide.
- October 31 – Typhoon Goni makes landfall in the Philippines, becoming the strongest landfalling tropical cyclone in history, displacing hundreds of thousands of people and killing dozens of people in the region.

November

- November 1
  - 2020 Moldovan presidential election: Former Prime Minister and Minister of Education Maia Sandu is elected as the 6th President of Moldova, becoming the first woman to ever hold the post.
- November 3 – November 7
  - 2020 United States presidential election: Joe Biden is elected as the 46th President of the United States, after remaining vote counts (November 7) come in from key states delayed by an influx of mail-in ballots caused by the pandemic, defeating and denying incumbent President Donald Trump a second term.
  - 2020 United States Senate elections take place, ending in an overall success for the Democratic party.
  - Hurricane Eta makes landfall in Nicaragua, killing over 100 people in Central America as a category 4.
- November 4 – The United States formally exits the Paris Agreement on climate change.

- November 8 – COVID-19 pandemic: The number of confirmed cases of COVID-19 passes 50 million worldwide.
- November 9
  - COVID-19 pandemic: The first successful phase III trial of a COVID-19 vaccine is announced by drug companies Pfizer and BioNTech, which is 90% effective according to interim results.
  - 2020 Nagorno-Karabakh War: Armenia and Azerbaijan sign a Russia-brokered ceasefire agreement.
- November 11 – COVID-19 pandemic: The Sputnik V vaccine is proven to be 92% effective against COVID-19 according to interim results.
- November 12 – Hong Kong pro-democracy lawmakers resign en masse, in response to four lawmakers' disqualification made by the government.
- November 15
  - The Regional Comprehensive Economic Partnership (RCEP) is signed by 15 Asia-Pacific countries to form the world's largest free-trade bloc, covering a third of the world's population.

- o NASA and SpaceX launch the SpaceX Crew-1 mission from Kennedy Space Center Launch Complex 39A to the ISS, the first operational flight of the Crew Dragon capsule.
- November 16
  - o COVID-19 pandemic: Moderna's mRNA vaccine is proven to be 94.5% effective against COVID-19 based on interim results, including severe illnesses. The vaccine has been cited as being among those that are easier to distribute as no ultra-cold storage is required.
  - o Hurricane Iota makes landfall in Nicaragua as a Category 4 hurricane just two weeks after Hurricane Eta made landfall, devastating the same areas.
- November 17 – COVID-19 pandemic: The number of confirmed cases of COVID-19 passes 55 million worldwide, with around a million cases recorded every two days on average.
- November 18 – COVID-19 pandemic: Pfizer and BioNTech complete trials on their COVID-19 vaccine, with an overall effectiveness rate of 95% without adverse events.

- November 19
    - The Brereton Report into Australian war crimes during the War in Afghanistan is released.
    - *Shuggie Bain* by Douglas Stuart wins the 2020 Booker Prize.
- November 22 – The United States withdraws from the Treaty on Open Skies.
- November 23 – COVID-19 pandemic: AstraZeneca's AZD1222 vaccine, developed in collaboration with Oxford University, is shown to be 70% effective in protecting against COVID-19. The efficacy can be raised to 90% if an initial half dose is followed by a full dose a month later, based on interim data.
- November 25 – COVID-19 pandemic: The number of confirmed cases of COVID-19 passes 60 million worldwide.
- November 27 – Iran's top nuclear scientist, Mohsen Fakhrizadeh, is assassinated near Tehran.
- November 28 – Koshobe massacre: Boko Haram jihadists attack a farm in Jere, Nigeria, killing at least 43 people.
- November 30
    - A penumbral lunar eclipse occurs; the last of four lunar eclipses in 2020.

- o Protein folding, one of the biggest mysteries in biology, is solved by AlphaFold, an artificial intelligence algorithm developed by DeepMind.
- o COVID-19 pandemic: Moderna files an application for Emergency Use Authorization in the United States after its vaccine achieved an efficacy of 94.1% from full trials without safety concerns. It also plans to do the same in EU soon.

December

- December 1
    - COVID-19 pandemic: Pfizer and BioNTech announced an Emergency Use Authorization application to the European Medicines Agency.
    - The Arecibo Telescope of the Arecibo Observatory collapses, just weeks after the announcement of its planned demolition.
- December 2
    - COVID-19 pandemic: The United Kingdom approves Pfizer-BioNTech's BNT162b2 vaccine, being the first country in the world to do so.
    - Three activists in Hong Kong were jailed for their roles in the 2019–20 Hong Kong protests, with Joshua Wong getting the heaviest at 13.5 months.
- December 3 – The UN Commission on Narcotic Drugs votes to remove cannabis from a list of dangerous drugs in recognition of its medical value, although some controls will remain.
- December 4

- COVID-19 pandemic: The number of confirmed cases of COVID-19 passes 65 million worldwide, with the global death toll exceeding 1.5 million. Figures reflect that, in the last week, over 10,000 people worldwide have died on average every day, with one death every nine seconds. According to the World Health Organization, COVID-19 had caused more deaths in 2020 than tuberculosis in 2019, as well as four times the number of deaths than malaria.
  - Somali Civil War: The United States announces its withdrawal from the conflict over the next month.
- December 5 – COVID-19 pandemic: Russia begins mass vaccination against COVID-19 with the Sputnik V candidate.
- December 6 – The 2020 Venezuelan parliamentary election takes place.
- December 8
  - COVID-19 pandemic: The United Kingdom becomes the first nation to begin a mass inoculation campaign using a clinically authorised, fully

tested vaccine, Pfizer–BioNTech COVID-19 vaccine. Margaret Keenan, 90, becomes the first person in the world to get the Pfizer jab outside of the vaccine's trial.

- Nepal and China officially agree on Mount Everest's actual height, which is 8,848.86m.

- December 10
    - COVID-19 pandemic: The United States and Saudi Arabia approve the Pfizer–BioNTech COVID-19 vaccine for emergency use, while Argentina approves Sputnik V.
    - Western Sahara conflict, Arab–Israeli conflict: Israel and Morocco normalise diplomatic relations. Simultaneously, the United States reaffirms its previous recognition of Moroccan sovereignty over the Western Sahara and announces plans to build a consulate there.
    - France: End of Nicolas Sarkozy corruption trial.

- December 11 – The European Union agrees to reduce greenhouse gas emissions by 55% over the next decade.
- December 12
    - COVID-19 pandemic: The number of confirmed cases of COVID-19 passes 70 million worldwide.
    - Bhutan and Israel normalise diplomatic relations.
- December 14
    - COVID-19 pandemic: The United States and Canada begin mass vaccination with the Pfizer–BioNTech COVID-19 vaccine. In addition, Singapore approves the Pfizer–BioNTech COVID-19 vaccine, with other companies to provide vaccines progressively.
    - Sudan–United States relations: The United States removes Sudan from its list of state sponsors of terrorism.
    - Turkey–United States relations: The United States places sanctions on Turkey in retaliation for their purchase of a S-400 missile system from Russia, making the first time they have sanctioned a NATO ally.

- - A total solar eclipse is visible from parts of the South Pacific Ocean, southern South America, and the South Atlantic Ocean.
- December 15 – The International Criminal Court accuses the Philippines of crimes against humanity in its war on drugs.
- December 16 – The United States formally designates Switzerland and Vietnam as being currency manipulators.
- December 18
  - - Media outlets report that astronomers have detected a radio signal, BLC1, apparently from the direction of Proxima Centauri, the closest star to the Sun. Astronomers have stated that this and other, yet unpublished, signals, are thought to likely be "interference that we cannot fully explain" and that it appears to be among the two strongest candidates for a radio signal humanity received from extraterrestrial intelligence so far.
  - - COVID-19 pandemic: The number of confirmed cases of

> COVID-19 passes 75 million worldwide.
> - COVID-19 pandemic: The United States approves Moderna's vaccine for emergency use, the second brand available there.

- December 20 – COVID-19 pandemic: A highly infectious new strain of SARS-CoV-2 spreading in Europe and Australia provokes international border closures.
- December 21
  - COVID-19 pandemic: 36 cases are reported on the Base General Bernardo O'Higgins Riquelme in the Chilean Antarctic Territory, marking the first infections in Antarctica, the last continent to report infections.
  - A great conjunction of Jupiter and Saturn occurs, with the two planets separated in the sky by 0.1 degrees. This is the closest conjunction between the two planets since 1623.
- December 23 – COVID-19 pandemic: Canada approves Moderna's vaccine, the second country to do so.
- December 24

- o The United Kingdom and the European Union agree to a comprehensive free trade agreement prior to the end of the transition period.
- o COVID-19 pandemic: Sinovac's vaccine reached a rate of 91.25% efficacy in trials in Turkey.
- December 27 – COVID-19 pandemic: The number of confirmed cases of COVID-19 passes 80 million worldwide.
- December 29 – The 2020 Petrinja earthquake with a magnitude of 6.4 strikes Croatia, killing seven and injuring more than 20.
- December 30 – COVID-19 pandemic: The United Kingdom approves AstraZeneca-Oxford's vaccine, the second one available. The vaccine is easier to store as it only requires normal fridge temperatures, making distribution easier.
- December 31 – The transition period following the United Kingdom's exit from the European Union on 31 January 2020 expires.

2021

198

January

- January 1 – The African Continental Free Trade Area comes into effect.
- January 4
  - A British judge blocks the extradition of Julian Assange to the United States, while Mexico offers him political asylum.
  - The border between Qatar and Saudi Arabia reopens.
- January 6 – Supporters of President Donald Trump attack the United States Capitol, disrupting certification of the 2020 presidential election and forcing Congress to evacuate. Five people die during the riot, including a police officer and a woman who is shot and killed inside the Capitol building. The event is classified as a domestic terrorist attack and draws international condemnation.
- January 10 – Kim Jong-un is elected as the General Secretary of the ruling Workers' Party of Korea, inheriting the title from his late father Kim Jong-il, who died in 2011.
- January 13 – In Lyon, France, the first transplant of both arms and shoulders is performed on an Icelandic patient at the Édouard Herriot Hospital.
- January 14 – The 2021 Ugandan general election is held.
- January 15

- o The Lao People's Revolutionary Party elects Thongloun Sisoulith as its new General Secretary, replacing retiring chief Bounnhang Vorachith. Sisoulith is elected for a five-year term as top leader in Laos.
  - o COVID-19 pandemic: The global death toll from COVID-19 passes 2 million.
- January 20 – Joe Biden is inaugurated as the 46th President of the United States, becoming the oldest individual to hold the office.
- January 22 – The Treaty on the Prohibition of Nuclear Weapons, the first legally binding international agreement to comprehensively prohibit nuclear weapons, comes into effect.
- January 24 – 2021 Portuguese presidential election: Incumbent president Marcelo Rebelo de Sousa is reelected.
- January 26 – COVID-19 pandemic: The number of confirmed COVID-19 cases exceeds 100 million worldwide.
- January 29 – COVID-19 pandemic: The European Union invokes Article 16 of the Northern Ireland Protocol following a row over COVID-19 vaccine supplies before reversing the decision.

- January 31 – Nguyễn Phú Trọng is re-elected for a third five-year term as the General Secretary of the Communist Party of Vietnam.

February

- February 1
  - A coup d'état in Myanmar removes Aung San Suu Kyi from power and restores military rule leading to widespread demonstrations across the country·
  - Kosovo officially establishes diplomatic ties with Israel and announces plans to open an embassy in Jerusalem.
  - COVID-19 pandemic: The number of vaccinations administered worldwide exceeds 100 million.
- February 3 – Canada becomes the first country to designate the Proud Boys as a terrorist organisation.
- February 4 – President Joe Biden announces that the United States will cease providing weapons to Saudi Arabia and the United Arab Emirates (UAE) for use in the Yemeni Civil War.
- February 9
  - COVID-19 pandemic: A joint WHO–China investigation into the source of the outbreak concludes. Investigators deem a Wuhan laboratory leak to be "extremely unlikely", with a

> "natural reservoir" in bats being a more likely origin.
>
> - The UAE's uncrewed *Hope* spacecraft becomes the first Arabian mission to successfully enter orbit around Mars.

- February 13–17 – A major winter storm kills at least 136 people and causes over 9.9 million power outages in the U.S.
- February 18 – NASA's Mars 2020 mission (containing the *Perseverance* rover and *Ingenuity* helicopter drone) lands on Mars at Jezero Crater, after seven months of travel.
- February 19 – The United States officially rejoins the Paris Agreement, 107 days after leaving.
- February 20 – 2020–21 H5N8 outbreak: 7 people test positive for H5N8 bird flu at a poultry farm in southern Russia, becoming the first known human cases.
- February 22 – COVID-19 pandemic: The United States becomes the first country to surpass 500,000 deaths from the virus.
- February 24 – COVID-19 pandemic: Ghana becomes the first country to receive vaccines through the COVAX vaccine-sharing initiative.
- February 25
  - COVID-19 pandemic: The global death toll from

COVID-19 surpasses 2.5 million.

- o The Armenian military calls for prime minister Nikol Pashinyan to resign. Pashinyan accuses the military of attempting a coup d'état.

March

- March 5 – COVID-19 pandemic: Moldova becomes the first country in Europe to receive vaccines through COVAX.
- March 6 – Pope Francis meets with Grand Ayatollah Ali al-Sistani in Najaf, Iraq. It is the first-ever meeting between a pope and a grand ayatollah.
- March 7 – Switzerland becomes the seventh European nation to ban the wearing of the burqa in public, joining Austria, Denmark, France, Belgium, Latvia, and Bulgaria.
- March 17 – The Dutch general elections for the House of Representatives of the Netherlands take place.
- March 19 – North Korea severs diplomatic ties with Malaysia due to its citizens being extradited to the United States to face money-laundering charges. Malaysian authorities order North Korean officials to leave the country in 48 hours.
- March 20 – Turkish President Recep Tayyip Erdoğan announces his country's withdrawal from the Istanbul Convention, the first country to do so.
- March 21 – Clashes in Apure between Colombian FARC dissidents and the Venezuelan Armed Forces cause at least eight casualties, as well as displacing 4,000 Venezuelans.

- March 23
    - The Israeli general elections take place, the fourth Knesset election in two years.
    - *Ever Given*, one of the largest container ships in the world, runs aground and obstructs the Suez Canal, disrupting global trade. The ship is freed on March 29.
- March 25 – COVID-19 pandemic: The number of vaccinations administered worldwide exceeds 500 million.

April

- April 2 – Russia warns NATO against sending any troops to aid Ukraine, amid reports of a large Russian military build-up on its borders.
- April 4
    - The 2021 Bulgarian parliamentary election takes place.
    - At least 167 people in Indonesia and 42 people in East Timor are killed after Cyclone Seroja strikes the island of Timor.
- April 9 – Roscosmos launches the Soyuz MS-18 mission, carrying three Expedition 65 crewmembers to the International Space Station.
- April 11
    - Peru holds a general election.
    - Iran accuses Israel of "nuclear terrorism" and vows revenge after a large explosion destroys the internal power system of the Natanz uranium enrichment plant.
    - Hideki Matsuyama wins the 2021 Masters Tournament, becoming the first man from Japan to win a major golf championship.
- April 13

- - Japan's government approves the dumping of radioactive water of the Fukushima Daiichi Nuclear Power Plant into the Pacific Ocean over the course of 30 years, with full support of the International Atomic Energy Agency. The decision is opposed by China, South Korea, and Taiwan.
  - The Johnson & Johnson COVID-19 vaccine is paused over causing rare blood clots.
- April 15 – Scientists announce they successfully injected human stem cells into the embryos of monkeys, creating chimera-embryos.
- April 17
  - - COVID-19 pandemic: The global death toll from COVID-19 surpasses 3 million.
    - The Czech government announced that the Russian GRU was responsible for the blast of two ammo warehouses in Vrbětice in 2014. Subsequently, 18 Russian diplomats and alleged spies were expelled.
    - The Soyuz MS-17 mission concludes, returning three

crewmembers of Expedition 64 to Earth from the International Space Station.

- April 18
  - Twelve football clubs, including three from the La Liga and leading clubs from the Premier League and Serie A, agree to join a new breakaway European Super League, prompting international condemnation. Two days later, following major protests from supporters, other clubs and politicians, Manchester City withdraw from the league; this prompts all the remaining Premier League clubs and three others to do the same.
  - The 2021 Cape Verdean parliamentary election takes place.
- April 19
  - NASA's *Ingenuity* helicopter, part of the Mars 2020 mission, performs the first powered flight on another planet in history.
  - Raúl Castro resigns as First Secretary of the Cuban Communist Party, ending

> more than 62 years of rule by the Castro brothers in Cuba.

- April 20 – Idriss Déby, President of Chad, is killed in clashes with rebel forces after 30 years in office. The constitution is suspended and a Transitional Military Council is established to govern the country for 18 months.
- April 21 – COVID-19 pandemic: With global case numbers approaching a second peak, India reports 315,000 infections within 24 hours, the highest one-day tally recorded anywhere in the world to date.
- April 22 – World leaders mark Earth Day by hosting a virtual summit on climate change, during which more ambitious targets for greenhouse gas emission reductions are proposed, including a 40% cut by 2030 for the United States.
- April 23
    - SpaceX launches the Crew-2 mission, carrying four crew members of Expedition 65 and 66 to the International Space Station aboard Crew Dragon *Endeavour*.
    - UEFA announces that due to a lack of guarantees regarding spectators caused by the COVID-19 pandemic, Aviva

Stadium in Dublin, Ireland would be removed as a tournament host for the UEFA Euro 2020.

- April 24
    - Following an international search and rescue effort, the Indonesian navy reports the sinking of KRI *Nanggala* with 53 crew members, the largest loss of life aboard a submarine since 2003·
    - COVID-19 pandemic: The number of vaccinations administered worldwide exceeds 1 billion. Half of these doses have been administered in just three countries (the United States, China and India).
- April 25 – Albania holds parliamentary elections.
- April 27 – India receives its first foreign aid shipments following the country's destructive COVID-19 second wave.
- April 28
    - At least 55 people are killed and nearly 50,000 more are displaced in one of the most serious clashes in Central Asia following border disputes between Kyrgyzstan and Tajikistan.

- o The European Union approves the EU–UK Trade and Cooperation Agreement, governing the relationship between the EU and UK after Brexit.
  - o Protestors rally in major Colombian cities against increased taxes and healthcare reforms proposed by President Iván Duque Márquez, resulting in police violence and the deaths of dozens of protestors, which is condemned by the United Nations and Human Rights Watch.
- April 29
  - o COVID-19 pandemic: The number of confirmed COVID-19 cases exceeds 150 million worldwide.
  - o The China National Space Administration launches the first module of its *Tiangong* space station, named *Tianhe*, beginning a two-year effort to build the station in orbit.
- April 30 – In Israel, 45 people are killed and another 150 injured in a crowd crush at a religious festival on Mount Meron.

May

- May 2 – The SpaceX Crew-1 mission ends, returning four crew members of Expedition 64 and 65 to Earth from the International Space Station aboard Crew Dragon *Resilience*.
- May 5 – SpaceX successfully flies, lands, and recovers a Starship prototype for the first time, after four unsuccessful previous attempts.
- May 11 – 2021 Israel–Palestine crisis: Israel hits the Gaza Strip with airstrikes as Hamas increases rocket fire. This occurred after Israel began displacing Palestinians in the Sheikh Jarrah neighbourhood of East Jerusalem.
- May 14 – The China National Space Administration lands its *Zhurong* rover at Utopia Planitia on Mars, making China the fourth country to land a spacecraft on the planet and only the second to land a rover.
- May 15 – Fighting between Israeli forces and Palestinian militants continues to escalate, as the death toll exceeds 150. An Israeli airstrike destroys a high-rise office building in Gaza occupied by Associated Press, Al Jazeera, and other media outlets.
- May 18–22 – The Eurovision Song Contest 2021 is held in Rotterdam, Netherlands, after the cancellation of the 2020 contest due to the COVID-19

pandemic. The 2021 contest is won by Italian entrants Måneskin with the song "Zitti e buoni".

- May 20 – Following international pressure, and nearly 250 deaths, Israel agrees to a ceasefire deal to end the conflict with Gaza militants, effective the next day at 2:00 AM local time.
- May 23 – Ryanair Flight 4978 is forced to land by Belarusian authorities to detain Roman Protasevich.
- May 24 – A coup d'état in Mali removes interim President Bah Ndaw and the acting Prime Minister, Moctar Ouane, from power and restores military rule leading to the country being suspended from the Economic Community of West African States and the African Union, as well as France suspending its military operations in the country.
- May 26
    - Shell becomes the first company to be legally mandated to align its carbon emissions with the Paris climate accord, following a landmark court ruling in the Netherlands.
    - The 2021 Syrian presidential election is held.
- May 29 – Chelsea beats fellow English club Manchester City in the final 1–0 to

become the champions of the UEFA Champions League for the second time.

215

June

- 2 June – The 2021 Israeli presidential election is held, and won by Isaac Herzog. In order to remove Prime Minister Benjamin Netanyahu from power, Naftali Bennett agrees to form a coalition with the Israeli opposition as a rotation government that will come to take effect after eleven days.
- 5 June – The G7 agrees on a global minimum corporate tax rate of 15% intended to prevent tax avoidance by some of the world's biggest multinationals.
- 7 June – The *Juno* spacecraft performs its only flyby of Jupiter's moon Ganymede, the first flyby of the moon by any spacecraft in over 20 years.
- 9 June
  - The 2021 Mongolian presidential election is held.
  - The Legislative Assembly of El Salvador passes legislation to adopt Bitcoin as legal tender in the country, becoming the first country to adopt the cryptocurrency alongside the U.S. dollar.
- 10 June – An annular solar eclipse is visible from Canada, Greenland, the North Pole, and the Russian Far East.
- 11 June–11 July – The UEFA Euro 2020, hosted by 11 different countries, is

held, and is won by Italy after beating England on penalties.

- 11 June–13 June – World leaders meet at the 47th G7 summit, hosted by the United Kingdom, with topics of discussion including the COVID-19 pandemic, climate change, and the corporate taxation of multinationals.
- 12 June – The 2021 Algerian legislative election is held to elect all 407 seats in the People's National Assembly.
- 13 June – Benjamin Netanyahu, the longest-serving prime minister of Israel, is voted out of office; Naftali Bennett and Yair Lapid are sworn in as Prime Minister of Israel and as Alternate Prime Minister of Israel, respectively.
- 13 June–10 July – The 2021 Copa América, hosted behind closed doors by Brazil, is held, and is won by Argentina.
- 17 June – The China National Space Administration sends its first three astronauts to occupy the Tiangong Space Station, the country's first space station.
- 18 June – The 2021 Iranian presidential election is held.
- 20 June – 2021 Armenian parliamentary election: Acting PM Nikol Pashinyan wins the country's snap election, with his Civil Contract party gaining 54% of the vote.
- 23 June – 2021 ICC World Test Championship Final: New Zealand wins

the 2019–2021 ICC World Test Championship.

- 24 June – Surfside condominium collapse: A portion of the Champlain South Towers condominium building collapses in Surfside, Florida, United States, leaving 98 people dead. One survivor was pulled from the wreckage while 35 others were evacuated from the uncollapsed section of the building.
- 25 June – Derek Chauvin is convicted and sentenced to 22 years and 6 months in prison, for the murder of George Floyd and for starting the national and international protest. Despite this, the civil unrest still goes on.
- 28 June – Tigray War: The Tigray Defense Force seizes the Tigrayan capital Mekelle shortly after the Ethiopian government declares a ceasefire.
- 29 June – COVID-19 pandemic: The number of vaccinations administered worldwide exceeds 3 billion.

July

- 3 July – Over 130 wildfires, fuelled by lightning strikes, burn through Western Canada following a record-breaking heatwave in North America that results in over 600 deaths.
- 5 July – More than 1,000 Afghan soldiers flee to neighboring Tajikistan after clashing with Taliban militants.
- 7 July – Assassination of Jovenel Moïse: Haitian President Jovenel Moïse is shot to death at 1:00 am local time in his home. First Lady Martine Moïse is injured and hospitalized.
- 8 July – COVID-19 pandemic: The number of deaths from COVID-19 surpasses 4 million.
- 10 July–1 August – The 2021 CONCACAF Gold Cup is held in, and is won by, the United States.
- 11 July
  - Thousands of Cubans, most of them young, attend a rare anti-government protest in San Antonio de los Baños to protest the increased food and medicine shortages brought on by the COVID-19 pandemic.
  - Moldova holds a parliamentary election, with the Party of Action and

       Solidarity (PAS) obtaining a majority of seats.

- o Bulgaria holds a parliamentary election, with the party There Is Such a People (ITN) leading.

- 12 July – 2021 European floods: Heavy rain causes flooding in the border region of Germany and Belgium, resulting in 229 deaths, including 184 in Germany, 42 in Belgium with 1 person still missing there, and 2 in Romania. The event is attributed to a slowed jetstream caused by climate change.

- 13 July – After the Supreme Court declares his incumbency unconstitutional, KP Oli is succeeded by Sher Bahadur Deuba as 43rd Prime Minister of Nepal.

- 18 July – An international investigation reveals that spyware sold by Israel's NSO Group to different governments is being used to target heads of state, along with thousands of activists, journalists and dissidents around the world.

- 19 July

  - o Blue Origin successfully conducts its first human test flight, with a reusable New Shepard rocket delivering four crew members into space including its founder Jeff Bezos.

- o Leftist schoolteacher Pedro Castillo is confirmed as President of Peru over a month after the 2021 Peruvian general election.
  - o Day of Hajj: Women are permitted to attend without a male guardian (*mehrem*) provided they go in a trustworthy group.
- 23 July–8 August – The 2020 Summer Olympics were held in Tokyo, Japan. They were originally scheduled for 24 July–9 August 2020, but were postponed due to the COVID-19 pandemic.
- 23 July – The Court of Appeal of Samoa deemed the swearing-in of Fiamē Naomi Mataʻafa and her government as constitutional, ending a three-month constitutional crisis.
- 25 July – Tunisian president Kais Saied formally takes power in the country, suspending the parliament and sacking the prime minister.
- 28 July – The first direct observation of light from behind a black hole is reported, confirming Einstein's theory of general relativity.
- 29 July
  - o Roscosmos' *Nauka* laboratory docks with the International Space Station following a protracted seventeen-year

development and launch on 21 July. Hours after docking, a malfunction of its thrusters causes a temporary loss of control of the station, spinning it up to 45 degrees from its normal orbital attitude.

- The oil tanker *Mercer Street* is attacked off the coast of Oman.

August

- 3 August
  - The oil tanker *Asphalt Princess* is hijacked off the coast of the United Arab Emirates.
  - Wildfires in Greece begin.
- 4 August
  - 2020 Summer Olympics: Belarusian sprinter Krystsina Tsimanouskaya is given political asylum in Poland through a humanitarian visa after attempts by the Belarus Olympic Committee to repatriate her against her will.
  - COVID-19 pandemic: The number of confirmed COVID-19 cases surpasses 200 million worldwide.
- 5 August – Tigray War: The Tigray Defense Forces seize the UNESCO World Heritage Site of Lalibela.
- 9 August – The Intergovernmental Panel on Climate Change releases the first part of its Sixth Assessment Report, which concludes that the effects of human-caused climate change are now "widespread, rapid, and intensifying".
- 12 August – The 2021 Zambian general election is held.

- 14 August – A 7.2-magnitude earthquake strikes Haiti, killing more than 2,500 people.
  - UK coalition forces assist a child during an evacuation at Hamid Karzai International Airport, Kabul
- 15 August – 2021 Taliban offensive: The Taliban capture Kabul; the Afghan government surrenders to the Taliban.
- 24 August–5 September – The 2020 Summer Paralympics were held in Tokyo, Japan. They were originally scheduled for 25 August–6 September 2020, but were postponed due to the COVID-19 pandemic.
- 26 August – 2021 Kabul airport attack: At least 182 people are killed, including 13 U.S. service members, in a suicide bomb attack at Kabul airport.
- 27 August – The United States launches an airstrike that it claims killed the Islamic State member who was believed to have planned the Kabul airport bombings. However, the U.S. Defense Department later acknowledged that the strike instead killed ten civilians, including seven children, and that no terrorists were killed.
- 29 August – Hurricane Ida strikes New Orleans, Louisiana, USA, after having caused devastation in Venezuela.
- 30 August

- o The UN Environment Programme announces that leaded petrol in road vehicles has been phased out globally, a hundred years after its introduction.
- o The United States withdraws its last remaining troops from Hamid Karzai International Airport, Kabul, ending 20 years of operations in Afghanistan.

September

- 5 September – 2021 Guinean coup d'état: Guinea's President Alpha Condé is detained by an elite military unit led by a former French legionnaire, Lt. Col. Mamady Doumbouya, claiming to have seized power.
- 7 September – El Salvador becomes the first country in the world to accept Bitcoin as an official currency.
- 13 September
  - Prime Minister Ismail Sabri Yaakob and Anwar Ibrahim, the leader of the main Malaysian opposition coalition Pakatan Harapan, sign a confidence and supply agreement ending the 18-month political crisis that has led to the fall of two successive governments in Malaysia.
  - The 2021 Norwegian parliamentary election is held.
- 14 September
  - North Korea demonstrates two short-range ballistic missiles that land just outside Japan's territorial waters; and then only hours later South Korea demonstrates its first

- submarine-launched ballistic missile.
  - o The inaugural season of the UEFA Europa Conference League, the third tier of European club football, kicks off with Israeli club Maccabi Tel Aviv winning 4–1 against Armenian club FC Alashkert.
- 15 September
  - o AUKUS: A trilateral security pact between Australia, the United Kingdom, and the United States is formed, to counter the influence of China. This includes enabling Australia to build its first nuclear-powered submarine fleet.
  - o Several ministers of the Argentine president Alberto Fernández's cabinet resign after the government's defeat in the primary elections, triggering a political crisis in the country.
- 16 September – Inspiration4, launched by SpaceX, becomes the first all-civilian private spaceflight, carrying a four-person crew on a three-day orbit of the Earth. Sian Proctor becomes first female commercial astronaut spaceship pilot

and Hayley Arceneaux becomes first astronaut with a prosthesis.

- 19 September – The 2021 Russian legislative election is held, with the United Russia party winning nearly 50% of the vote.
- 20 September – The 2021 Canadian federal election is held, with Justin Trudeau and the Liberal Party retaining a minority government.
- 25 September – The 2021 Icelandic parliamentary election is held.
- 26 September – The 2021 German federal election is held, with Olaf Scholz and the Social Democratic Party beating out the CDU/CSU coalition.

October

- 1 October – The 2020 World Expo in Dubai begins. Its opening was originally scheduled for 20 October 2020 but was delayed due to the COVID-19 pandemic.
- 3 October – The International Consortium of Investigative Journalists and assorted media partners publish a set of 11.9 million documents leaked from 14 financial services companies known as the Pandora Papers, revealing offshore financial activities that involve multiple current and former world leaders.
- 4 October – Fumio Kishida becomes the 100th Prime Minister of Japan, succeeding Yoshihide Suga.
- 5 October
    - Microsoft releases the desktop operating system Windows 11.
    - Roscosmos launches the Soyuz MS-19 mission, which carries an Expedition 66 crewmember and two Channel One Russia personnel to the International Space Station. The two Channel One crew will perform principal photography on the film *Vyzov* aboard the station.

- 6 October – The World Health Organization endorses the first malaria vaccine.
- 6–10 October – The 2021 UEFA Nations League Finals is held in Italy, and is won by France. They were originally scheduled for 2–6 June 2021, but were moved following the rescheduling of UEFA Euro 2020 to June and July 2021 due to the COVID-19 pandemic.
- 8–9 October – The 2021 Czech legislative election is held, with the main opposition coalition alliance of SPOLU and Pirates and Mayors gaining a legislative majority.
- 9 October – Sebastian Kurz announces his resignation as Chancellor of Austria as a result of a corruption probe launched against him.
- 16 October – The Lucy spacecraft is launched by NASA, the first mission to explore the Trojan asteroids.
- 17 October–14 November – The 2021 ICC Men's T20 World Cup is held in the United Arab Emirates and Oman, and is won by Australia.
- 23 October – Colombia's most wanted drug lord, Dario Antonio Úsuga, whose Gulf Clan controls many smuggling routes into the US and other countries, is captured by Colombia's armed forces.
- 24 October – The 2021 Uzbek presidential election is held.

- 25 October – The Sudanese military launches a coup against the government. Prime Minister Abdalla Hamdok is placed under house arrest. President Abdel Fattah al-Burhan declares a state of emergency and announces the dissolution of the government.
- 31 October
    - The 2021 Japanese general election is held, with Fumio Kishida and the Liberal Democratic Party along with its coalition partner Komeito retaining a majority government.
    - 31 October–13 November – The 2021 United Nations Climate Change Conference is held in Glasgow, after being postponed in 2020 due to COVID-19. A deal is agreed by world leaders, which includes a "phasedown" of unabated coal power, a 30% cut in methane emissions by 2030, plans for a halt to deforestation by 2030, and increased financial support for developing countries.

November

- 1 November – COVID-19 pandemic: The number of recorded deaths from COVID-19 surpasses 5 million.
- 5 November
  - Tigray War: The Tigray People's Liberation Front forms a coalition with eight other rebel groups with the aim of defeating the Ethiopian government "by force or by negotiations."
  - A crowd crush at the Astroworld Festival hosted by Travis Scott in Houston, Texas, kills 10 people and causes 300+ injuries.
- 11 November – SpaceX launches the Crew-3 mission, carrying four Expedition 66 crew members to the International Space Station.
- 14 November
  - The 2021 Argentine legislative election is held.
  - The 2021 Bulgarian general election is held.
- 16 November – Russia draws international condemnation following an anti-satellite weapon test that creates a cloud of space debris, threatening the International Space Station.
- 21 November – The 2021 Chilean general election is held.

- 24 November
    - NASA launches the Double Asteroid Redirection Test (DART), the first attempt to deflect an asteroid for the purpose of learning how to protect Earth.
    - Magdalena Andersson resigns as Prime Minister-elect of Sweden hours after the Riksdag voted her in as Sweden's first female Prime Minister. She was due to take office on 26 November. Instead, she takes office on 30 November.
- 24 November–12 December – Magnus Carlsen beats Ian Nepomniachtchi in the 2021 World Chess Championship. Magnus has been World Chess Champion since 2013.
- 26 November – COVID-19 pandemic: The World Health Organization convenes an emergency meeting in Geneva amid concerns over Omicron, a highly mutated variant of COVID-19 first identified in South Africa that appears more infectious than Delta.
- 30 November–18 December – The 2021 FIFA Arab Cup is held in Qatar, and is won by Algeria.

- The Governor-General of Barbados Sandra Mason is sworn in as the country's first President.
- 30 November – Barbados becomes a republic on its 55th anniversary of independence while remaining a member of the Commonwealth of Nations.

December

- 4 December – The 2021 Gambian presidential election is held and incumbent president Adama Barrow is reelected.
- 6 December – The United States announces a diplomatic boycott of the 2022 Winter Olympics in Beijing in response to China's human rights record. Canada, the United Kingdom, and Australia join shortly after.
- 9 December
    - A truck crash in Chiapas, Mexico, kills 55 migrants who were being smuggled in it from Guatemala through Mexico to its border with the United States.
    - 9–10 December – The Summit for Democracy, a virtual summit, is hosted by the United States "to renew democracy at home and confront autocracies abroad".
- 10–11 December – A late season tornado outbreak occurs in the Southern and Midwestern United States, causing major damage and killing at least 94 people. One of the longest-tracked tornadoes in history occurred, which impacted western Kentucky, particularly Mayfield.

- 11 December – New York City FC defeats the Portland Timbers at Providence Park in Portland, Oregon 5–3 on penalties after a 1–1 draw, and win MLS Cup title for the first time in their history.
- 12 December
    - The 2021 New Caledonian independence referendum is held.
    - Max Verstappen won his first Formula One World Championship and the first for a Dutch driver, driving for Red Bull Racing at the Abu Dhabi Grand Prix.
- 16 December – Typhoon Rai, also known as Typhoon Odette, hits the Philippines and caused destruction to agriculture, establishments, and houses, and caused many injured and deaths.
- 19 December
    - The 2021 Hong Kong legislative election, originally scheduled for 6 September 2020 but postponed due to the COVID-19 pandemic, is held.
    - The second round of the 2021 Chilean presidential election is held; leftist candidate Gabriel Boric is elected President.

- o Artistic conception of the James Webb Space Telescope.
- 25 December – NASA, ESA, the Canadian Space Agency and the Space Telescope Science Institute launch the James Webb Space Telescope, the successor of the Hubble Space Telescope.

Author's Note

'*Anoroc- Tres*' is the third and the final part of the '*Deception series*'. There are eleven books in this series, three main books and eight referral books. With this book this series ends here.

Hope my readers had a good time reading my "*Deception series*".

Thank you!

240

Other books from the series.

Deception series
ANOROC:
UNO
DORIAN
SNOWDEN

Anoroc: Uno

In an era where social media are ruling, the freedom to speak about anything and many things has been brutally and forcefully suppressed without knowingly.

Exposing off-screen things can be a crime in this era.

This book is conspiracy-oriented, the entire 'Deception series' is itself dedicated to the conspiracy face of Corona and references to prove they are not some fabricated fictional story.

Deception series
ANOROC:
DUO
DORIAN
SNOWDEN

Anoroc: Duo

When the current generation is more toward social media the author took a step back and shared sensitive information by means of books instead of getting censored on social media. This book is an eye-opener; the perspective in which Corona has been described is not something the majority of people think about.

What makes the book even more interesting is the facts and figures the author put forth to solidify the statements and connect the points, showing nothing is by accident but a staged show.

Will the author be able to unfold the behind the curtain scene entirely?